WHAT YOUR COLLEAGUES ARE

Gregory C. Hutchings, Jr. and Douglas S. Reed ... thoughtful, important, and timely book. It is ...... reading for school leaders who value racial equity enough to put it into practice and for policymakers and advocates as well.

—Jonah Edelman
Co-Founder and Executive Officer, Stand for Children,
Portland, OR

Getting Into Good Trouble at School is a must-read for anyone interested in the future of American education. Drs. Hutchings and Reed identify six essential steps. If absorbed and applied, these steps will serve as waypoints in the pursuit of critical change supporting all students in constructing an antiracist school system.

—Robert E. Baker
Dean and Professor, College of Education
and Human Development,
Fairfax, VA

This book is a powerful and thoughtful analysis of the enduring impact of institutional racism upon American education. Hutchings and Reed combine deeply personal reflections and anecdotal narratives about how racism has impacted minority students. The book is a strong endorsement for using strategic planning and the continuous improvement process to build a transformed system that is aligned, mission- and vision-driven, culturally responsive, and personalized.

—John L. Brown
Writer and Researcher in Residence, AASA,
The School Superintendents Association,
Alexandria, VA

This is a book that every educator and every parent should read. It is clear, comprehensive, and tells the unsettling truth about racism in public schools in America. It lays out specific steps to once and for all dismantle the racism that continues to plague our society and deny BIPOC children their right to an equitable education.

—Mary-Frances Winters
President, The Winters Group, Inc,
Author of *Black Fatigue: How Racism Erodes
the Mind, Body and Spirit*

Hutchings and Reed offer a direct approach to confronting systems of racism. Through sharing personal experiences, a deep knowledge of the existing literature, and data informed practices, the authors offer a call to action that requires assessing current practices, establishing an intentional strategic plan, and being courageous enough to implement the plan.

—Tammi Dice
Interim Dean, Darden College of Education and
Professional Studies,
Old Dominion University,
Norfolk, VA

Here, finally, are authors with the courage to lay out concrete steps school leaders can take to encourage antiracist schools to grow and thrive. Gregory C. Hutchings, Jr. and Douglas S. Reed offer six steps to dismantle systemic racism in American schools while getting into "good trouble" to help Americans live out the full meaning of "all men (and women) are created equal."

—James Harvey
Executive Director, National Superintendents Roundtable,
Seattle, WA

This courageous text provides testimonies of lived experiences interwoven against a historical backdrop of the impact of racism on our educational system. It takes the reader on a journey to understand how to advance an equity lens and become an antiracist educator. The authors artfully challenge the status quo while the guided questions force you to reflect and act.

—Dawn Williams
Dean, Howard University School of Education,
Washington, DC

As educators are doubling down on efforts to reimagine student-centered, forward-leaning public education, *Getting Into Good Trouble at School* points out why it's essential to boldly advocate for the vast number of U.S. children who should be receiving the services that they are entitled to. I congratulate the authors for casting a shining light on the principles of educational equity and social justice.

—Daniel A. Domenech
Executive Director, AASA,
The School Superintendents Association,
Alexandria, VA

Getting Into Good Trouble at School

Getting Into Good Trouble at School

A Guide to Building an Antiracist School System

Gregory C. Hutchings, Jr. and
Douglas S. Reed

Foreword by Pedro A. Noguera

FOR INFORMATION:

Corwin
A SAGE Company
2455 Teller Road
Thousand Oaks, California 91320
(800) 233-9936
www.corwin.com

SAGE Publications Ltd.
1 Oliver's Yard
55 City Road
London EC1Y 1SP
United Kingdom

SAGE Publications India Pvt. Ltd.
B 1/I 1 Mohan Cooperative Industrial Area
Mathura Road, New Delhi 110 044
India

SAGE Publications Asia-Pacific Pte. Ltd.
18 Cross Street #10-10/11/12
China Square Central
Singapore 048423

President: Mike Soules
Vice President and Editorial
   Director: Monica Eckman
Senior Acquisitions Editor: Tanya
   Ghans
Content Development Manager:
   Desirée A. Bartlett
Editorial Assistant: Nyle De Leon
Production Editor: Tori Mirsadjadi
Copyeditor: Exeter Premedia Services
Proofreader: Dennis Webb
Typesetter: Exeter Premedia Services
Cover Designer: Scott Van Atta
Marketing Manager: Morgan Fox

Printed in Canada

ISBN: 9781071857014

This book is printed on acid-free paper.

22 23 24 25 26 10 9 8 7 6 5 4 3 2 1

Contents

Foreword

The global pandemic has confronted educational leaders with numerous unprecedented challenges and controversies, heightening US political tumult while at the same time sharply revealing long-endured inequities in educational resources and opportunities. Throughout the continuing public health threat, superintendents, school boards, and college administrators have found themselves grappling with new, unprecedented controversies and challenges: pushback against mask and vaccine mandates, student learning loss, and an alarming rise in mental health needs. At the same time, the pandemic has created an even greater awareness of the existing and deepening inequities that threaten the well-being of children and families—in particular, persistent and durable racial disparities in education—as well as the emergence of bitter debates over how to teach about the history of race and racism in American society.

To navigate these issues while keeping an eye firmly focused on student support and outcomes, educational leaders must acquire a new set of skills. Resourcefulness, tact, diplomacy, as well as an ability to communicate to an array of constituencies that are more divided than ever before, while still managing the operations of schools and keeping the needs of students at the forefront. When Gregory C. Hutchings became the superintendent of Alexandria City Public Schools (ACPS) in 2018, he challenged the school district and the community to focus its attention on racial disparities in education, putting racial equity at the center of his work. While doing so, he encountered Professor Douglas S. Reed's work on the historical origins of racial inequality within Alexandria's schools and invited him to serve on Hutchings's 100-day transition team as he took the reins at ACPS. Their partnership eventually led to the publication of this book.

I describe school leaders like Hutchings as "breakthrough" leaders. I use this term because rather than simply treading water and waiting for the controversies to subside, or allowing controversies to result in organizational paralysis, Hutchings confronts the challenges facing his district, his schools, and community head-on. He draws upon the insights he has gained as an experienced educator and the knowledge he has acquired from others to find a way to continue to make a difference for his students and communities. Armed with the historical insights of Reed's earlier work, Hutchings asked Alexandria to come to terms with the reality of its racial past—and present. This work is not easy and it challenges many accepted practices within education. It requires transformation and deep skills of understanding, planning, and leadership. This book is about how to organize and design that transformation and how to understand, plan, and lead for racial equity in schools.

Gregory C. Hutchings and Douglas S. Reed draw on the lessons of civil rights icon and former member of Congress, John Lewis, to inspire their work. Undertaking the transformations urged by Hutchings and Reed will, undoubtedly, produce trouble, but it is Good Trouble, the kind that Lewis described as essential for advancing racial justice in the United States. Like John Lewis, Hutchings and Reed are guided by values and insights that are critical for "breaking through" during these challenging times. For educational leaders who are seeking ways to breakthrough their own obstacles and challenges, the lessons shared by Hutchings and Reed will be invaluable.

We are in the midst of a "new normal." Crises such as school shootings, threats against educators who feel students have a right to learn about America's history of racism, and new uncertainties created by political polarization and climate change will test and challenge education leaders in the years ahead. Hutchings and Reed have provided us with a perspective on how we can approach these challenges, both those we have known and those we have yet to encounter. For that, we should all be grateful that we have a guide in how to make "good trouble" in education.

—Pedro A. Noguera
Emery Stoops and Joyce King Stoops Dean
Distinguished Professor of Education
USC Rossier School of Education

Preface

GET INTO GOOD TROUBLE, NECESSARY TROUBLE

Since 2020, our nation has confronted a dual pandemic. In March 2020, due to COVID-19 schools across the United States closed their doors and pivoted to virtual learning overnight, exacerbating our already severe educational disparities. As schools later transitioned to hybrid learning as well as concurrent teaching in classrooms, the social, emotional, and academic learning of young people across the nation suffered enormously.

In addition to the global COVID-19 pandemic, the United States continues to experience a centuries-long racial pandemic. The brutal murders of George Floyd, Breonna Taylor, Ahmaud Arbery, and countless others whose lives were senselessly taken due to the color of their skin, along with racial tension across the country, intensified and deepened protests of our tightly woven patterns of systemic racism. Harsh racism has been a central feature of the history of the United States for over 400 years, but the events of 2020 and 2021 have brought about a national reckoning with race. Part of that reckoning requires calling out the extremists among us: Americans watched the January 6, 2021, insurrection at the US Capitol by rioters and malicious citizens who irrationally believed that the election of our 46th president of the United States, Joseph Biden, was flawed and somehow stolen from the former president Donald Trump. Covert and overt racism in the United States reached its highest level since the civil rights movement, even as millions protested globally for an end to police violence against communities of color.

This dual pandemic sparked a national conversation about the need to finally dismantle systemic racism in the United States. In spite of these struggles, educators across the country continue to strive for racial equity within schools. Indeed, these ruptures of "normalcy" have generated the momentum for transformative changes in school and society to address the inequities we see around us. The twin crises of COVID-19 and racial injustice afford an opportunity for schools and school systems to begin their journey to becoming antiracist. This is why we were so compelled to write this book. The title of our book was inspired by a powerful quote from US Representative John Lewis, "Do not get lost in a sea of despair. Be hopeful, be optimistic. Our struggle is not the struggle of a day, a week, a month, or a year, it is the struggle of a lifetime. Never, ever be afraid to make some noise and get in good trouble, necessary trouble." Therefore, the title *Getting Into Good Trouble at School: A Guide to Building an Antiracist School System*. To eliminate racial inequities in schools and school systems across the country, we must have the boldness and courage to cause Good Trouble at school.

WHAT SCHOOL LEADERS WILL GET OUT OF THIS BOOK

This book will provide school leaders with a unique perspective of two authors who have led very different walks of life. One author is an African American man who is tired of being forced to overcome adversity while being African American in the United States and the other author is a Caucasian man who acknowledges his White privilege and strives to be a coconspirator for changing the racial equity narrative in the United States. One author grew up in a homogeneous community in the Pacific Northwest while the other author grew up in the city of Alexandria, a metropolitan community near the US capital. Though the authors have different life experiences, both have attained terminal degrees in their fields from prestigious universities and both are obsessively committed to dismantling systemic racism in education. Our goal is to help you build an antiracist school or school system. To do that, we draw on our life experiences, our expertise in diversity, equity, inclusion and the study of race, our working knowledge of school systems, and the passion and common sense needed to achieve racial justice in schools. The result is, we hope, a kind of guidebook that provides encouragement, context, and concrete actions needed for antiracist schools to grow and thrive.

SIX STEPS TO BUILDING AN ANTIRACIST SCHOOL SYSTEM

1. Know Your History to Rewrite Your Future (Chapter 2)
2. Commit to Racial Equity (Chapter 3)
3. Dismantling Tracking and Within-School Segregation (Chapter 4)
4. Making School Discipline Different From Policing (Chapter 5)
5. Implement Strategic Thinking and Planning (Chapter 6)
6. Choose Good Trouble: Be a Bold and Courageous Antiracist School Leader (Chapter 7)

SIX STEPS TO BUILDING AN ANTIRACIST SCHOOL SYSTEM

In this book, we identify six steps that are integral components of building an antiracist school system: (1) You and your community must know your history as a school system and tell the stories that have been left untold; (2) Your school system needs to understand that committing to racial equity is integral to academic excellence; (3) Racial equity means dismantling tracking and within school segregation that limits the educational experiences of Black, Indigenous, and People of Color (BIPOC) students; (4) Transforming school disciplinary practices is necessary to break the criminalization of youth, particularly BIPOC youth; (5) You need to engage the project of racial equity through a strategic analysis of your school system and the development of a strategic plan for racial equity; (6) You need to lead with boldness and courage as you undertake the work of racial equity within your school system.

We have identified these six steps through our experiences in school systems and through a deep review of research on schooling, race, and educational transformation. These steps reinforce and support one another and are best seen as cornerstones of the new kind of school system you are seeking to build: an antiracist school system.

FEATURES AND BENEFITS OF THIS BOOK

Each chapter follows a schema to support the reader's understanding of the journey to becoming antiracist. The *Guiding Principles* at the beginning of each chapter provide the reader with the key guiding principles of the chapter to set the stage for their reading experience. Because this is a practical book meant to guide busy administrators in implementing antiracist practices, each chapter contains a *Tips* section briefly summarizing an implementable action step. The *Reflective Questions* at the end of each chapter help the reader to develop personal reflections and to identify organizational insights, initial steps, long-range possibilities, and anticipated barriers and challenges. We offer these Guiding Principles, Tips, and Reflective Questions with the conviction that achieving equity in schools begins with a clear understanding of the contexts of schooling as well as concrete and actionable steps that parents, teachers, students, principals, administrators, and school system leaders can take in their own daily work with schools. This is a book for both understanding and action. In the chapters you will also find *examples where these actions steps have worked successfully* in school systems across the United States.

THE TERMS WE USE AND WHY

Throughout the book, we use the term Black, Indigenous, and People of Color (BIPOC) to emphasize the injustices that continue to impact both Black and Indigenous people in the United States. In 2020, the term BIPOC became more widely used amidst the nation's protests of police brutality against Black people and the resurgence of the Black Lives Matter movement. We have chosen to use BIPOC throughout the book to refer to Black persons who identify as of African or Caribbean descent; Indigenous persons who are descendants of natives who inhabited North America before it was stolen by European settlers; and people of color (people who are not White). We understand that this term may be unfamiliar to some readers and therefore wanted to provide a clear definition and purpose within this book.

Similarly, we follow the American Psychological Association's style of capitalizing Black and White, when referring to the specific experiences and identities of individuals of those races and the characteristics of institutions. In so doing, we acknowledge the social construction of these categories and the processes by which both individuals and institutions come to possess a racial identity. To speak of "White schools" highlights (albeit subtly) that the racial homogeneity of those schools is not accidental or natural in a way that labeling them "white schools" does not.

We define *antiracism* as a commitment and obligation to recognize and actively challenge patterns of behavior and outcomes that persistently harm Black, Indigenous, or people of color. Integral to this definition is the recognition that these patterns of behavior and outcomes may or may not be the product of individually held beliefs about race, racial identity, or racial supremacy or inferiority. That is, these patterns and outcomes may arise and be maintained even when individuals are not overtly engaging in racist behavior. As a result, we define *antiracist school leader* as someone who embraces a commitment and obligation to recognize and actively challenge patterns of behavior and outcomes that persistently harm BIPOC students; the antiracist school leader recognizes that systemic racism within the educational system emerges even when individuals are not engaged in overtly racist behavior or hold overtly racist views. Moreover, an antiracist school leader takes proactive steps to undo systemic racism within school systems, as well as challenge overtly racist actions and views.

USE THIS GUIDE TO BECOME AN ANTIRACIST SCHOOL LEADER

We hope that this book will provide the reader with the necessary guidance and support to enhance their equity-driven and antiracist educational leadership that will transform the lives and well-being of all children, but especially BIPOC students in our schools across the country. The 1954 *Brown v. Board of Education* Supreme Court decision was supposed to transform public education across the United States by integrating our schools and affording Black children the same educational opportunities as their White counterparts. However, the second Supreme Court ruling in the *Brown v. Board of Education* case in 1955 included the phrase "with all deliberate speed" as it addressed the required pace of racial change in Southern schools. Unfortunately, today we are still seeing far too much deliberation and far too little speed in our quest for racial justice in schools. Indeed, the attack on critical race theory within schools is an effort to stop all discussion of race and racial inequities and the ways that schools and school officials create and perpetuate those inequities. Now is not the time to stop talking about race. In fact, the opposite is true: Now is the time to be bold and courageous while unapologetically striving to become antiracist. This is your step to changing the narrative on race relations across the United States of America, and we commend you for starting, continuing, or validating your journey to becoming an antiracist school or school system.

Acknowledgments

While our names may be on the cover, this book has emerged from the encouragement, inspiration, and generosity of so many people in our lives and our work. First and foremost, it is important to acknowledge the Black, Indigenous, and People of Color who have endured tragedy, adversity, struggles, accomplishments, and triumphs over the last few centuries. We stand on their shoulders and reap advantages from their courage and boldness throughout history. We want to acknowledge the late civil rights activist and US Representative, John R. Lewis, for his courageous leadership and famous quote, "Never, ever be afraid to make some noise and get in good trouble," that inspired us to write this book. Additionally, we would like to acknowledge Corwin for believing in our vision for this book, especially our editors, Ariel Curry and Desirée Bartlett, for their guidance, support, and push when needed throughout the writing process.

ACKNOWLEDGMENTS BY GREGORY C. HUTCHINGS, JR.

I am so grateful for my God almighty who has literally ordered my steps throughout my life and has given me the gift of servitude and advocacy for those who are not always given a seat at the table. My spiritual faith guides my life and equips me to continue this journey of antiracism. I would like to acknowledge my wife, Cheryl, who continues to be my life partner, best friend, and greatest supporter until the end of my time on this Earth. My wife is the best gift that God has given me and our love is like fine wine that gets better over time. I've become my "best self" due to her unconditional love, support, encouragement, and keeping me grounded when the helium from the world tries to lift me into the stratosphere. Our children, Micah and Gregory III, are a product of our covenant and will continue our legacy of spreading love on this Earth. I continue to strive for excellence and will always strive to be a good example for both of them. My life's work is to ensure that they get the opportunity to live a full life without systemic racism.

I want to acknowledge my first teacher who is my mother, Shari Thomas, who raised me to be my authentic self and taught me one of my greatest gifts, which is selflessness and being proud to be an African American man in America. My mom always believes in me and encourages me to do my best at all times. Also, I truly want to thank my first public school teacher in kindergarten, Mrs. Dorothy McKenzie, who told me at five years old that I could be the first Black president of the United States of America and I actually believed her. She instilled in me the confidence that started my life's journey of serving others and I'm forever grateful for the seeds she planted at the beginning of my educational journey that afforded the foundation I have in my life today.

Thank you to my coauthor, Dr. Douglas S. Reed, who has literally become one of my best friends while writing this book. Our reflections and discourse on racism has ignited a continuous flame for dismantling systemic racism in schools across America. You are truly a brilliant educator who will be my thought partner for decades to come. I would like to acknowledge one of my mentors, Dr. Pedro A. Noguera, who encouraged me to speak my truth. You believed in my vision for writing this book when I was entertaining the thought and your encouragement truly empowered me to get the book completed. I want to acknowledge my dear friend, Dr. John L. Brown, who takes every call and helps me whenever I need him, especially when I had moments of writer's block while writing the book. Your guidance, support, and assistance throughout this book journey is greatly appreciated. Also, a huge thank you to Alexandria City Public Schools (ACPS) for helping to mold me into the person that I am today. I'm grateful for the learning experiences that I've had throughout my life in ACPS. I'm so blessed to be able to serve the community that served me during my school days.

I want to acknowledge my spiritual and inspirational leaders who literally give me the fortitude to keep taking action to dismantle systemic racism while fulfilling my life's purpose. Thank you to Dr. Jawanza K. Colvin for being my "forever Pastor," spiritual brother, and dear friend over the years. You continue to be my spiritual leader and I'm forever grateful for you being in my life. Also, Dr. Billy K. Cannaday, for being my "forever mentor" and my self-assigned God-father. You gave me a chance to begin my school leadership journey and have literally been there throughout my entire educational career as a supporter, motivator, and listener. You never tell me what to do and are great at asking me the right questions to help me discover the answers. I continue to admire you and appreciate the love and guidance you've provided throughout my career.

Finally, I must acknowledge my iPhone and yes, I'm acknowledging a technology device. I literally wrote this entire book on my iPhone instead of a computer because it afforded me the opportunity to write anywhere and at any time without disturbing my wife at 3 a.m. in the bed. It has been the best thumb typing in my life and I look forward to writing many more books.

ACKNOWLEDGMENTS BY DOUGLAS S. REED

This book emerged in the wake of one of the largest social uprisings in US history, arguably in global history, and in the midst of a global pandemic that has taken millions of lives. Both of these events have changed history—and changed my views on many things. I would like to acknowledge the contributions and labor of those who built a democratic movement for racial justice in the 21st century. Their ongoing work has been an inspiration for me. I would also like to acknowledge the work and dedication of millions of teachers who, throughout the pandemic, have sought to inspire and connect with students in incredibly challenging circumstances. Your work and persistence have amazed me and continue to inspire me.

I am a political scientist by training, but over the past decade my work has shifted more squarely into the field of education. Part of the reason for that has been my work with Professor Sabrina Wesley-Nero, here at Georgetown University, first with the undergraduate Program in Education, Inquiry, and Justice and now with the MA Program in Educational Transformation. Much of what I have learned in education comes from my work and collaboration with her and I thank her deeply for sharing that knowledge with me. I also thank her for her friendship and deep wisdom. I would also like to thank my other colleagues in Educational Transformation, past and present: Priya Goel LaLonde, Crissa Stephens, Kristin Sinclair, Christa Pluff, and Anne Musica. Your knowledge and insights have built a remarkable program and have helped me to better understand the landscape of education, race, and equity.

I want to thank Dr. Gregory C. Hutchings, Jr. for suggesting that we write this book together. Little did I know that our collaboration would yield not only the book you hold in your hands but also a deep and lasting friendship. It is said that friendships and coauthorship do not always mix, but for me the act of writing a book together and talking through the challenges of race and racial justice have forged a greater understanding of myself and the world we live in, as well as a friend and writing partner. So, thank you for that gift and for your patience as well when progress slowed. I'm also thankful that I don't work for you so that you can't fire me when I miss a deadline. I want to thank Angel Reed (no relation) and Rashaud Hannah for their outstanding work as research assistants on this project.

Also, I would like to thank my family. My wife Denise Brennan has been a steadfast supporter of this project and I thank her for patience while I slipped away to work on it. During the worst of the pandemic, we were fortunate to have our grown children,

Emily and James, return to live with us for a few months. It was truly a respite from a raging storm to share time with them again, as adults, and see what wonderful human beings they have become. I must also thank those that we turned to when the pandemic forced us all to pull inward: Marybeth McMahon, Ben Simon, Edie Brashears, Charlotte Mooney, and Christopher Jones. Your friendship means more than I can say.

PUBLISHER'S ACKNOWLEDGMENTS

Corwin gratefully acknowledges the contributions of the following reviewers:

Jacqueline Arce
Deputy Head of Secondary
NIST International School
Bangkok, Thailand

Amanda E. Austin
Principal
Iberville STEM Academy
Rosedale, LA

Louis Lim
Vice Principal
Richmond Green Secondary School
Richmond Hill, Ontario, Canada

Jacie Maslyk
Educator-Presenter-Author
www.steam-makers.com
Pittsburgh, PA

Vernita Mayfield
President
Leadervation Learning LLC
Denver, CO

Lena Marie Rockwood
Assistant Principal
Revere High School
Revere, MA

Teresa Tung
Secondary School Principal
Hong Kong Academy
Hong Kong

About the Authors

Gregory C. Hutchings, Jr. is a nationally recognized educational leader, anti-racism activist, and adjunct professor who unapologetically advocates for Black, Indigenous, and People of Color and racial equity. He has over twenty years of combined educational experience as a teacher, school principal, central office administrator, superintendent, and college professor.

Dr. Hutchings is the chief executive officer and founder of an educational consulting firm, Revolutionary Ed, LLC. His life's work is educational service and dismantling systemic racism in schools across America. Dr. Hutchings was the 2018 recipient of the Joseph E. Hill Superintendent of the Year Award with the National Alliance of Black School Educators.

Dr. Hutchings earned his doctorate in educational policy, planning, and leadership from the College of William & Mary. He currently serves on numerous national boards and is an active member of Alpha Phi Alpha Fraternity, Incorporated. Dr. Hutchings is a native of Alexandria, Virginia, where he currently serves as the superintendent of Alexandria City Public Schools and resides with his wife and their two children.

Douglas S. Reed is a Professor of Government at Georgetown University, where he is the founding director of the MA Program in Educational Transformation. His research interests center on the politics of education, educational policymaking, federalism, and judicial politics. His current work focuses on legal notions of race, equality, and colorblindness and how educational policy can improve student outcomes by directly addressing the racial contexts and experiences of students.

He is the author of *Building the Federal Schoolhouse: Localism and the American Education State* (Oxford University Press, 2014) and

On Equal Terms: The Constitutional Politics of Educational Opportunity (Princeton University Press, 2001).

He has been a fellow at the Woodrow Wilson International Center for Scholars, an Advanced Studies Fellow at Brown University, and was named a Carnegie Scholar by the Carnegie Corporation as well as a National Academy of Education/Spencer Foundation Post-Doctoral Fellow. He earned his PhD from Yale University.

Introduction

How do teachers, students, parents, school leaders, and administrators build an antiracist school system? This book tackles that challenging question, from two distinct, but aligned, perspectives. The first perspective grows out of Dr. Gregory C. Hutchings, Jr.'s experiences of being a student, an administrator, and ultimately superintendent in a school district where race has long controlled the education that a student receives. The second perspective emerges from Dr. Douglas S. Reed's historical understanding of how that racist school system was built—brick by brick, policy by policy. Combined, we feel that these two perspectives can powerfully equip school leaders—teachers, administrators, and students—to demand and create not just a nondiscriminatory school but an antiracist one.

We believe that our understanding of what creates racist school systems and what creates antiracist school systems can be used as a powerful tool throughout the United States. Our hope is that this work can be used to recreate school systems, to commit them to antiracist practices and policies, and to finally grant the promise of a culturally rich and profound education to all students.

A distinctive aspect of this book is that it is coauthored by an African American man who was educated in Alexandria public schools and grew up to become its superintendent working to dismantle the racist practices and systems that he personally had to overcome as a student. Greg Hutchings's personal story in Alexandria's schools—and afterward—provides a vivid picture of ways that policies and practices structure the educational (and life) opportunities of Black, Indigenous, and People of Color (BIPOC) students in systemically racist ways. In the fall of 1992, just before Bill Clinton was elected president of the United States, Gregory Hutchings began his sophomore year at T. C. Williams High School, in Alexandria, Virginia.

Greg's Story

I remember the excitement and prestige of wearing the Titans logo on my T-shirt as I walked the halls of T. C. Williams. The high school sometimes felt like a session of the United Nations due to its cultural diversity and its status as the only high school in the city of Alexandria. Alexandria was—and is—a city of the haves and the have-nots, but it brought all of its students together in one building in high school. Despite that physical proximity of diverse students, Alexandria's educational system nonetheless divided students by race as it tracked students into courses.

I knew I was destined for college after high school, and I also knew that college preparatory courses were the key to fulfilling that destiny. Unfortunately, at the beginning of my sophomore year, the school administration enrolled me in classes that were not on the college track, taught by unmotivated teachers. On a typical day, my teacher would write the assignment on the board then sit and read the news-paper at his desk, not concerned whether students learned or even completed the assignment.

One day, while walking to the bathroom after being excused from class, I noticed that other classrooms seemed to be highly engaged. I heard student-led discussions, ideas being exchanged, and even some laughter. A light bulb went off in my head: I needed—and wanted—to be in a learning environment like that. I soon discovered these high-energy and rigorous classes were the Honors classes. My first thought was, "Well, sign me up" and I scheduled a meeting with my school counselor to be enrolled in the Honors class.

Unfortunately, the school counselor informed me that my test scores and grades were not good enough for Honors and therefore school policy did not permit me to enroll. I was devastated, but rather than accepting the school counselor's decision, I decided to ask my fellow classmates to sign a petition to allow me to enroll in the Honors class. I then had the audacity to take the petition signed by several students to the high school principal to request enrollment despite not meeting the course requirements.

To my surprise, the principal admired my determination and courage and walked me to the counseling department to enroll me in the Honors course. At that moment, I realized for the first time that my voice was powerful, and it is even more powerful when it is heard by someone willing to assist. My life's trajectory changed at that very moment and stirred my desire to be an advocate not only for myself but for others—especially those who are ignored. I graduated from T.C. in 1995 and headed to Old Dominion University (ODU) through early admissions by the support and encouragement of my senior year school counselor.

Despite my enthusiasm, my first year in college did not go well. ODU was a predominantly White institution with large lectures of at least 500 students. In my first year of college, I had a 1.2 GPA (Grade Point Average) and was placed on academic probation. I felt underprepared for college. I experienced imposter syndrome and began to feel guilty about being in college, asking myself why I was there. Even though I had enrolled in Honors classes during my high school years, I was not prepared for postsecondary education nor the independence that college afforded. At a time when I saw others ready to tackle the world, my self-esteem was low, and I felt like a failure.

I had friends who attended Hampton University and spent much of my time visiting them at Hampton. During my sophomore year, I decided to transfer to the prestigious, historically Black university. There, I saw another side of Black life in the United States. For the first time in my life, I was surrounded by Black students who were all on a mission to change the world. With Black professors and demanding classes, filled with predominantly Black students, Hampton is a college for the Black elite. It was the first time, outside of sitcoms like *The Cosby Show* and *A Different World*, that I saw Black students who had generational wealth, drove expensive cars, and had parents who were doctors or lawyers.

Hampton University generated in me a sense of pride that I had never felt before. I made the Dean's List for the three consecutive semesters that I was there. The message of Hampton—and historically Black colleges and universities (HBCUs) across the country—taught me powerful lessons: how to be a young Black man, to respect myself and my Black history—to even know my own family history. At Hampton, I had an epiphany that just like my White counterparts, I, too, deserved to be at the table and to have a voice in this country.

Those lessons were profoundly different from those I had at T. C. Williams, where my Black peers and I experienced poor or indifferent teaching, low expectations, and an oppressive culture inflicted by the mostly White teaching force. This dismissal of Black students and Black culture deprived me and my classmates the perspective that Hampton provided: serving witness to the talent, culture, and contributions that Black Americans provided to US history. T.C. had failed BIPOC students and neglected my untapped potential—and that of countless other BIPOC classmates.

Hampton undid that sense of discouragement and neglect. Though my time at Hampton University was short-lived, it was a pivotal and

(Continued)

powerful moment in my life. The eighteen months at Hampton gave me the confidence I needed to succeed as a Black man in our country. I decided to return to ODU to finish my "college race" with a newfound confidence and Black pride, thriving both academically and socially. I maintained a GPA of 3.0 or higher through graduation and joined the first Black collegiate Greek lettered fraternity, Alpha Phi Alpha Fraternity, Inc. I was proud to join the likes of Thurgood Marshall, Frederick Douglass, Martin Luther King, Jr., Jesse Owens, W. E. B. DuBois, Duke Ellington, Adam Clayton Powell, Jr., Dick Gregory, Cornel West, and other luminaries as an Alpha man. I later became the chapter president.

Fast forward twenty years: I am now the superintendent of Alexandria City Public Schools after earning my doctorate in education at the second oldest college in the United States, the prestigious College of William & Mary, and serving as the superintendent of Shaker Heights Public Schools, a trailblazing school system in Ohio.

While many things have changed for me, for BIPOC students too many constants remain. During my tenure as superintendent in two different states, I've spoken with countless BIPOC students whose school counselors discouraged them from enrolling in rigorous courses—just as I experienced in my high school years. One Black student shared that she reviewed her course options and wanted to enroll in an AP course, a common choice for students with college aspirations but less common for many BIPOC students. Her parents supported that choice and encouraged her to pursue her desire. To her frustration, her school counselor discouraged her from taking the class, indicating that it was a demanding, college-level course. Just as I had done long before her time, she persisted, and insisted that her school counselor approve her course selections. These efforts at schools across the United States to deny Black students a challenging and rich curriculum stretch across generations. This experience showed me once again how consistently school systems have discriminated against BIPOC student over time, even to the present day.

THE HISTORICAL AUDACITY AND POWER OF BLACK LIVES MATTER

In 2020, the Black Lives Matter (BLM) movement galvanized public opinion and motivated efforts to tackle racism directly. The

FIGURE 0.1 ● Black Lives Matter

Image by Patrick Behn from Pixabay

current efforts to tackle racism go beyond requests that White folks try not to discriminate or requests that society realize how White norms influence all our systems and institutions. The BLM movement has inspired current activists to tackle racism directly by demanding the dismantling of policies and practices that systematically and continuously disadvantage BIPOC lives. In schools, that means no longer tolerating ostensibly racially neutral policies that "just happen" to fall disproportionately on students of color. To be antiracist is to realize that racism doesn't just happen; it is systemically built and maintained.

The BLM movement has shown many White Americans what most Black Americans already knew: that the experiences of Whites within the criminal and social justice systems are vastly different from the experiences of people of color. The same is true of the educational system in the United States. While many individual teachers and administrators reach out to address the needs of BIPOC students, larger, systemic forces deny educational equity to BIPOC students. In other words, individual BIPOC students may benefit from caring educators who reach out to mentor or advocate for them. But those piecemeal efforts—as valuable and rewarding as they may be—are insufficient to address the scope of systemic racism in education. It's not enough for people like Greg's principal and senior year school counselor to take a shine to individual students, to allow one or two to take an honors course, or to help them with a college essay. What is needed is a systemic response that strategically targets the circumstances that give rise to the inequities in the first place. The point is not to help a few select students overcome the obstacles of systemic racism in education, the point is to remove systemic racism from education. White detractors will point to success stories of a few individual BIPOC students as "evidence" that systemic racism doesn't exist and that the system rewards talent and hard work. What is left out of these feel-good anecdotes is how comparable efforts by equally talented White and BIPOC students yield vastly different outcomes. Instead of telling stories of students who overcome adversity to succeed, we need to identify the elements of the educational system that routinely and repeatedly ensure that that BIPOC students are disproportionately represented among students who don't finish high school and those referred to the juvenile justice system, tracked into poorly taught classes with low expectations, and overrepresented among students identified with emotional or behavioral disturbances but underrepresented among students identified with a learning disability. And then we need to replace and repair those elements of the system.

> White detractors will point to success stories of a few individual BIPOC students as "evidence" that systemic racism doesn't exist, that the system rewards talent and hard work. What is left out of these feel-good anecdotes is how comparable efforts by equally talented White and BIPOC students yield vastly different outcomes.

Young people of color need what public education has offered to affluent White students for generations: exposure to a rich set of learning experiences, the presence of role models who look like them to build confidence, institutional support to identify and achieve their goals, a ready encouragement to thrive, a robust expectation that they will thrive, and ample resources to intervene if they are not thriving. Unfortunately, these are the specific areas that are lacking in our schools across the nation. The systemic racism that permeates public education crushes, both academically and personally, so many BIPOC students every year. While the creation of public schooling advanced the prospects of White US citizens, the wholesale neglect of schooling for their BIPOC counterparts left them to fend for themselves and, as a result, many grew convinced that they were unworthy or not good enough, despite their obvious talents and abilities.

THE HISTORICAL LEGACIES AND CONTINUITIES OF RACISM IN EDUCATION

The current pervasive achievement and opportunity gaps within schools and society are the results of historic and present-day efforts to keep BIPOC children inferior and oppressed, efforts that date back to Horace Mann's advocacy for common schooling in the 1830s and 1840s. When the organizers of a Black boycott of Boston's public schools called on Horace Mann repeatedly in the 1840s to condemn the segregation of White and Black students in Boston, Horace Mann refused, not wanting to jeopardize his efforts to gain more resources for White public education (Mabee, 1968). Into the 20th century, as Southern schools faced desegregation court orders, they closed Black schools and fired Black teachers to meet the minimum requirements of court-ordered desegregation, imposing costs on the communities least ready to bear those costs. Dr. Martin Luther King, Jr. once said, "Now I believe we ought to do all we can and seek to lift ourselves by our own bootstraps . . . but it's a cruel jest to say to a bootless man that he ought to lift himself by his own bootstraps. And many negroes, by the thousands and millions, have been left bootless as a result of all of these years of oppression" (King, 1967).

In our day, some leaders expect our BIPOC students to overcome adversity and to have the "grit" to engage in rigorous course-work (Duckworth, 2018); however, we ignore the generational oppression and institutional racism that continues to intention-ally marginalize people of color in the United States. In 1967, Stokely Carmichael and Charles V. Hamilton wrote

> When a black family moves into a home in a White neighborhood and it is stoned, burned or routed out, they are victims of an overt act of individual racism which most people will condemn. But it is institutional racism that keeps black people locked in dilapidated slum tenements, subject to the daily prey of exploitative slumlords, merchants, loan sharks and discriminatory real estate agents. The society either pretends it does not know of this latter situation, or is in fact incapable of doing anything meaningful about it. (Ture et al., 1967, p. 4).

This form of institutional and systemic racism still defines edu-cational experiences of BIPOC students and permeates public educational institutions across the United States. Acts of overt discrimination may be condemned in schools, but conditions of systemic racism are tolerated, indeed often fostered, by schools and their leaders. BIPOC students have known about these cir-cumstances and these excuses for generations; many in White society either claim to not know or to be incapable of doing anything meaningful in response. This book aims to show all Americans what can be done to redress systemic racism within schools and to urge us all to get into more than a little Good Trouble at our schools.

CHAPTER 1

Reimagining the Titans

GUIDING PRINCIPLES

1. Antiracist school leaders eliminate systemic racism by examining and changing the existing practices within schools that limit educational opportunity for BIPOC students.

2. Antiracist school leaders engage the voices of all stakeholders, especially BIPOC stakeholders, when drafting organizational strategies and school policies.

3. Antiracist school leaders unapologetically take action to dismantle systemic racism and they confront opposition and barriers when they inevitably arise.

4. Antiracist school leaders learn how to use strategies to achieve their vision of racial equity.

In 2000, Walt Disney Pictures released *Remember the Titans*, a biographical sports film that captured the courage, determination, and boldness of the late high school football coach Herman Boone. The film highlighted the trials and tribulations of consolidating three high schools in the city of Alexandria, Virginia, into one high school, T. C. Williams. It extols football as a unifying force that brought White and Black people together during the turmoil of integration. The film portrays Coach Boone as a tough-as-nails Black man who loved his family dearly and who had the audacity to challenge the White former head coach, Bill Yoast. It's a tearjerker and a rousing sports film, all rolled into a feel-good story of a community overcoming its history of bigotry. And that's precisely the problem with the film: it depicts a mythic story of racial healing that, for the most part, makes White people feel better about Black inequality and the meager efforts undertaken to redress that inequality.

The real story of why Alexandria merged its three high schools is more complicated than the version told in *Remember the Titans*. In 1965, as a brand-new high school (T. C. Williams) opened, Alexandria converted the Jim Crow-era all-Black Parker-Gray High School into a middle school and created high school attendance zones based on neighborhoods. The result was three officially desegregated high schools that mirrored the residential segregation of the city: Hammond High on the west side of town was virtually all-White. George Washington High School, on the east side and near the historically Black neighborhood of the Berg, had a Black enrollment of 25 percent, while the brand-new T. C. Williams, in the center of the city, enrolled roughly 12 percent Black students (Reed, 2014). Those enrollment figures proved to be highly unstable as White flight from desegregated schools on the east side of town drove up the percentage of Black students at George Washington High School, which quickly developed a reputation among Whites as the "Black" high school in Alexandria.

Tensions among students also grew, particularly as school leadership proved unable or unwilling to foster the relationships among students and staff that would overcome long histories of distrust between White and Black in Alexandria. In the fall of 1970, the city's schools were in turmoil. The murder of Robin Gibson in May 1970 by a 7-Eleven clerk who claimed Gibson had shoplifted some razor blades led to six consecutive nights of protests. In November 1970, a hung jury failed by an 11–1 vote to convict Gibson's murderer. Earlier that month, members of the American Nazi Party burned crosses on school grounds. These events seethed through Alexandria's high schools, galvanizing Alexandria's Black youth who demanded that a school system long accustomed to ignoring their needs actually address their demands, which ranged from a relaxed disciplinary policy to more Black teachers to more courses in Black culture and history. In the view of Superintendent John Albohm, racial conflict permeated the schools and the geographic division of the three high schools exacerbated those tensions. As the school board chair remarked later, disciplinary matters and poor morale "were tearing the system apart" (Reed, 2014, p. 75). Albohm's solution to these conflicts was to create one very big high school—which just happened to have a very good football team. In May 1971, the school board voted to merge the city's three high schools, effective that fall, sending the city's junior and seniors to T. C. Williams and the sophomores and freshman to the two former four-year high schools. The rest is cinematic history, marked by an undefeated season and a state football championship.

Although the film *Remember the Titans* ends at the conclusion of the 1971 high school football season, the story of racial conflict within Alexandria City Public Schools (ACPS) did not. While later conflicts may not have been as explosive, the racial tensions experienced in 1971 continued throughout the 1980s, 1990s, and 2000s—not only in the city of Alexandria and ACPS but nationwide as well. The Hollywood version of desegregation shows Black and White students, along with Black and White community members, overcoming their animosity to live together, if not peaceably then at least as a single community. As Denzel Washington, playing Coach Boone, told the players when he took them to the Gettysburg Battlefield, "I don't care if you like each other or not, but you will respect each other." The problem is that the Hollywood story of winning grudging respect, forged out of a common effort to achieve victory, has little to do with the reality of the deep disrespect many school systems, including ACPS, continue to hold for the educational opportunities of BIPOC students.

On its surface, the narrative of *Remember the Titans* echoes the same narrative that many BIPOC students in Alexandria (and across the nation) face as they attend one of the largest and most diverse high schools in the country. The surface equanimity and get-along attitudes of teenagers as they navigate the interpersonal relations and conflicts of adolescence are demonstrably better than it was in the late 1960s and early 1970s. But that superficial, Hollywood view does not show the systemic racism and racial disparities that remain to be dismantled. *Remember the Titans* captured the mythic qualities of integrating the T. C. Williams High School football team, but it did not show us truly integrated classrooms, curricula, and challenges. In reality, T. C. Williams—like many large high schools throughout the United States—is an intricate work of student racial segregation within an integrated building. Today, the students of color in ACPS are still isolated from their White peers through a form of modern-day de facto segregation, through programs like Advanced Placement, Dual Enrollment, Talented and Gifted programs, and special education.

> T. C. Williams—like many large high schools throughout the United States—is an intricate work of student racial segregation within an integrated building.

In the film and in real life, students and players sing T. C.'s fight song, "We are the Titans . . . the mighty mighty Titans." We've even seen police officers lead Black Lives Matter protesters in that cheer to show their solidarity. What that song fails to address, however, is that not all Titans are treated equally or equitably. Both implicit and explicit double standards exist for BIPOC students in ACPS and their White counterparts. But that's not unusual: achievement and opportunity gaps between White students and BIPOC students across the United States are pervasive and they have been since the inception of public education.

The barriers that deny Black students access to a high-quality education are numerous, ranging from course selection, to disciplinary systems, to over- (and under-) identification in special education, to pervasive beliefs about Black failure among mostly White teachers, beliefs that oppress and colonize the minds of BIPOC students. Unfortunately, US society appears to have accepted the myth that the color of your skin determines your destiny. In this book, we are unapologetic about exposing and confronting those who continue to perpetuate these unequal structures and inaccurate ideologies. By identifying these systems of injustice, and showing how schools can dismantle them, this book lays out what is necessary to finish the job started in *Remember the Titans*— the achievement of a truly equitable and antiracist school system.

ACPS is one of the most diverse school systems in the country with students from over 120 countries enrolled in the city's only public high school, which in April 2021 changed its name from T. C. Williams to Alexandria City High School. We can sing the school's fight song, *We Are the Titans*, but then we all go our separate ways once the game is over. Today, fifty years after three high schools merged, students experience achievement and opportunity gaps that are more pervasive than before. In 2019, all of T. C. Williams' National Merit Semi-Finalists were White—just as they were in 1971. Despite the growing diversity of T. C. Williams, the fact that highly visible leadership positions and high academic honors persistently accrue to only White students indicates that something is systematically excluding BIPOC students from these accolades. But students are not accepting this state of affairs. Just as in 1971, BIPOC students at T. C. are mobilizing and speaking out, through the Minority Student Achievement Network (MSAN), a national organization striving to diminish achievement and opportunity gaps in public school systems across the United States. Through these efforts, they are demanding that the school and school system leadership address these opportunity gaps and build a truly equitable school and school system. But the challenges are daunting.

CHALLENGES TO EQUITY AND INCLUSION

ADVANCED PLACEMENT

Consider Advanced Placement. Like most schools across the United States, the Advanced Placement (AP) courses at T. C.—which enable students to earn college credit while in high school—are filled, mostly, with White students and a few BIPOC students. When asked why they don't enroll more frequently in AP courses, BIPOC students often express not just feelings of exclusion or isolation in AP but describe explicit experiences of discrimination and oppression that drive them away. Often the rebukes from teachers and students center on assumptions about *who belongs in AP*, with the prevalence of White students defining a traditional WASPy classroom culture that is unwelcoming to BIPOC students. Moreover, until recently AP teaching assignments are frequently awarded to mostly White teachers, who often do little to engage BIPOC students, compounding their sense of isolation and lack of support. Why go where you're clearly not wanted?

DISCIPLINE STANDARDS AND PRACTICES

Zero tolerance discipline policies are part of a harsh discipline system that mirrors a prison mentality. Like criminal justice systems across the United States, school discipline policies often employ a double standard for BIPOC students compared to their White peers. When sanctions are leveled unequally for similar offenses—depending on the race of the perpetrator—BIPOC students lose access to learning, have their school record permanently marred, and receive the message that they are unwanted. Rather than rely on a punitive disciplinary process that feeds a school-to-prison pipeline (particularly for students of color), schools need to see discipline as an opportunity not to exclude students from schooling but to help form citizens of the future and to shape individuals who have an understanding of how their actions affect the community around them. A school discipline program anchored in restorative practices places students at the center of creating a vibrant and expressive community in which norms of behavior emerge from a sense of student belonging. Rather than demanding compliance and punishing students when they do not comply, a restorative practice program empowers students to regulate and enforce the norms of behavior that facilitate learning within a school. We see these programs as essential to ensuring racial justice within schools.

SCHOOLS ARE DESIGNED TO PERPETUATE INEQUALITY: A LOOK AT YESTERDAY AND TODAY

Despite the growing racial, ethnic, national, and linguistic diversity in US schools, the educational system in the United States seems to have only one template for student success and that template is clearly color-coded. School systems and practices in the United States were designed to boost and aid White students but thwart and obstruct BIPOC students. Many of those practices have not ended, despite the end of legally mandated segregation. One must know our nation's and our schooling history in order to not repeat it. When schools initially desegregated across the country, White educational leaders founded private schools to enable affluent White families to avoid racially mixed schools. At the same time, special education services and talented and gifted programs became indirect ways to keep BIPOC students and White students apart.

History seems to continue to repeat itself. In 2020, as the world confronted a global pandemic and schools remained closed, virtual learning became the new normal for public education. But many White families with financial means established learning pods to ensure that their children continued "on track," justifying the exclusive nature of in-person learning in the COVID era as essential childcare for two-career adults. These learning pods brought together small groups of kids to learn, collaboratively, in conjunction with online public schooling, often with privately hired tutors or teachers to facilitate these pods. Small, intimate, expensive, and likely of high quality, these learning pods simply exacerbated the most recent trends of declining support for public education.

Moreover, as parents hired tutors and teachers and drew on social networks and social capital to form learning pods, they explicitly worsened the divisive gap between the haves and have-nots. They also entrenched the color line in public education. Indeed, this learning model is not far removed from the concept of White flight during the integration of public schools in the 1960s and 1970s. We share this to emphasize that if we do not know our history of withdrawal and exclusion, then we are bound to repeat it. It is unconscionable that our public educational systems across the United States continue to not serve our BIPOC students well and in some cases not at all.

BECOME ANTIRACIST

It's time to change the narrative for public education across the United States, ensuring that all students regardless of their life's circumstances, zip code, race, gender, socioeconomic status, or educational ability are engaged in learning experiences that prepare them to become productive global citizens who attain success. The cessation of overtly racist practices is not enough to halt the pernicious effects of racism. We need, in the words of Ibram X. Kendi, to become antiracists—as teachers, school leaders, parents, and community members. Without taking on this perspective, efforts to create equitable school systems will fail. School systems across the country might strive to provide a safe learning environment where staff are culturally competent and diversity is supposedly embraced; however, without antiracism at the heart of this work, schools—and the legacy of racism within schools—will continue to oppress, misunderstand, and damage BIPOC students. We consistently hear our educators say they are not racist—especially our White educators. If no one is racist, why do we tolerate racist outcomes? We need more than just non-racists leading and teaching in schools; we need antiracist educators leading our schools and teaching our students.

The six steps outlined in the preface and each chapter of this book are not easy steps, but they are simple steps. Their simplicity, however, demands courage and boldness to first identify and then dismantle systemic and institutional racism in our public schools. And even though they are not easy, these steps are essential: educators determine the future of our country and, right now, they are nurturing and developing the next generation of leaders in the world—White and BIPOC. We have accepted the status quo in public education across the United States for far too long and the time is now to reject—unapologetically—racist acts, behaviors, practices, policies, people, and ideologies that contaminate our educational philosophies and practices. Take the pulse of your school system. This checklist might help you get a sense of how closely your school or district adheres to antiracist principles.

IS YOUR SCHOOL AN ANTIRACIST SCHOOL?

☐ Are White and BIPOC students suspended at the same rate?

☐ Do low-income students receive the same educational experience as higher income students?

- ☐ Are BIPOC students identified as in need of special services for emotional disabilities at the same rate as White students?

- ☐ Are BIPOC students identified for learning and reading disabilities, such as dyslexia at the same rate as White students?

- ☐ Are you taking actions to identify and address issues that negatively affect BIPOC students?

- ☐ Are you eradicating any practices that disproportionately inflict trauma on BIPOC students?

- ☐ Do you have a representational number of BIPOC teachers and staff among your faculty?

- ☐ Do all teachers have the cultural competence to engage BIPOC students in their classrooms?

- ☐ Are you taking actions to address racial inequities in your school?

Today, the evidence is increasingly clear that public school systems harm BIPOC students by not being antiracist, by inflicting trauma on them throughout their educational experiences, and by ignoring horrific racial inequities in our schools. If you answered "no" to any of the items on the checklist and have not done something to dismantle these practices, then you have not demonstrated the courage and boldness needed to change this narrative in public education. Tackling these issues requires that all of us, as individuals, make a commitment to racial equity in our public schools, in our own school systems, and across the nation.

The issue is not only one of social justice but of fundamental public health. The fact is that racism imposes psychological damage and traumatic experiences on BIPOC students. A meta-analysis review of 138 studies in the *International Journal of Epidemiology* reported that self-reported experiences of racism or discrimination among adults was highly associated with negative mental health outcomes for people of color, with 72 percent of the studies showing a negative relationship. Over a third of the studies found that individuals suffered negative physical health outcomes when they reported having experienced discrimination or racism (Paradies, 2006). These findings align with other studies that show adverse childhood experiences (known as ACEs) affect both a child's education and life outcomes. The Centers for Disease Control (CDC) and Kaiser

Permanente collaboratively studied the effects of traumatic experiences during childhood for roughly 13,500 adults and the impacts of these experiences on the health status, incidence of disease, and prevalence of risky behaviors as adults. The study found, among other things, that persons who experienced four or more ACE factors had a four- to twelvefold increased risk for alcoholism, drug abuse, depression, and suicide attempt, when compared to respondents who had no ACE factors (Felitti et al., 1998).

If we regard school-based discrimination and racism as an adverse childhood experience (as we should), these studies suggest that there are lifelong mental and physical health implications when children are exposed, over the long term, to schools that systematically deny them opportunities to learn and to advance based on their race. Of course, these adverse experiences of racism are not limited to childhood; BIPOC students experience ongoing stressors as adults and over their life span—with profound health implications. One study of the experiences of over 1,300 African American women found that higher perceptions of on-the-job racial and ethnic discrimination were linked to significantly higher levels of job-related stress, which has long been shown to have clear health implications. Importantly, women with higher levels of education perceived greater levels of discrimination. Whether experienced as an adult in the workplace or as a student in the classroom, racism and discrimination produce systemic health effects for people of color, throughout their lives.

In 1758, Carl Linnaeus, known as the father of taxonomy, developed the first classification system for the human race. Specifically, he used a color scheme to identify what we refer to today as different races. His groupings included four categories: white European, dark Asiatic, red American, and black Negro. Linnaeus even applied "descriptive" labels to the "characteristics" of the types of humans he identified: white people as hopeful; dark people as sad and rigid; red people as irascible; and black people as calm and lazy. Over 100 years ago, W. E. B. Du Bois objected to the practice of viewing race as rooted in biological differences of Black and White people rather than in the social and cultural differences of human beings. As one learns about the historical contexts of race, the negative images and descriptors of BIPOC students come into immediate focus; these terms and images are still projected into the world. These images and stereotypes and characterizations sustain and expand the racist ideology that permeates public educational institutions across our country. The ludicrous myth that race is rooted in biological differences among human beings has unfortunately shaped how we treat BIPOC students in public education in the United States—and not in a good way.

In schools across the United States, educational tracking has been central to widening the achievement gap. In our day (back in the 1970s and 1980s), elementary students were assigned to the Bluebirds or Redbirds reading group. Today, our public educators have gotten savvier with tracking and now use practices such as pull-out services, self-contained classrooms, advanced level courses, and international academies to place students in classrooms based on their ability levels. These educational practices unfortunately have wide currency in public education and some public school systems have even convinced families and educators that these practices are best for their children, especially BIPOC children.

Generating the political will to take action is not sufficient, however. To dismantle systemic racism in public education across the United States, we must think and plan strategically in order to overcome adversity and obstacles. While the moral case for meeting all students' social, emotional, and academic needs is abundantly clear, in reality, any school or school system division that unapologetically takes action to dismantle systemic racism will confront opposition. At this juncture, you must be ready to relentlessly make what John Lewis called "good trouble" in order to prevail. Strategic thinking and strategic planning are the most important components of dismantling systemic racism. Political savvy will enable you to navigate the tough road ahead.

A strategic thinker pursuing antiracism must be self-reflective and always strive to understand the justification and rationale for a particular decision. You must be able to answer the questions, "What is compelling about this decision?" Not, "Why are you *forced* to make this decision?" But "What makes this decision necessary?" That reasoning, that compelling why, tells you and others what is at stake in your decision-making process. As you find your compelling why, you must also anticipate the reactions, obstacles, outcomes, and potential shortcomings you will encounter. Strategic thinking requires self-efficacy and competency. But most of all, to strategically plan how to construct an antiracist school or school system, you must build a coalition of allies and coconspirators who can support you while you navigate the troubled waters of systemic racism. This book will provide insight on how to establish your coalition and refine your practice through strategic thinking and planning.

> To strategically plan how to construct an antiracist school or school system, you must build a coalition of allies and coconspirators who can support you while you navigate the troubled waters of systemic racism.

Strategic planning with courage and boldness will provide your organization with the road map to an antiracist school system and also unapologetically remove barriers and set high ambitions for the system. These ambitious, yet attainable goals will fuel the success of your students. In order to dismantle systemic racism and become an antiracist school or school system, one must ensure that the organization's mission, vision, and core values are aligned with the organization's belief that all students will learn, as well as emphasize the importance of eliminating both achievement and opportunity gaps in public education. Racial equity must be at the heart of the organization's day-to-day operations and planning.

Strategic thinking and strategic planning are intertwined and must be at the forefront of dismantling systemic racism in public education. You cannot combat systemic racism without a strategic plan, and that plan requires you—and your school system—to commit to ensuring all students are treated equitably. You will confront relentless naysayers and those who oppose the antiracist movement. Thinking your way, strategically, through leadership and planning your desired outcomes, without apologies, are essential attributes of creative leadership. The current landscape of racist schooling requires astute and nimble strategic planning and thinking; without those skills, you will lack the tools needed to construct a public education system free of racism, oppression and inequity.

PLAN OF THIS BOOK

CHAPTER 1: GET INTO GOOD TROUBLE

This chapter has given you a sense of our background and experiences, as well as our perspectives on racism in public education and a sense of our commitments. We envision this book as a guide to help you create not just a non-racist school or school system but an antiracist one. We will tackle six steps of this work: (1) knowing your history; (2) committing fully to racial equity; (3) dismantling tracking and within school segregation; (4) transforming school discipline practices; (5) engaging in strategic thinking and planning; and (6) leading with boldness and courage. These steps form the foundation of an antiracist school system.

CHAPTER 2: KNOW YOUR HISTORY TO REWRITE YOUR FUTURE

In Chapter 2, we address the importance of knowing your history—both locally and nationally—and understanding the narrative of racism that has shaped the experiences of students and teachers in your school. Knowing the stories of an explicitly racist past and connecting them to the experiences and actions of students and teachers and leaders of today enables us to better understand and confront the racism that persists within our educational institutions. Uncovering these counter-narratives and connecting them to current contexts of education contextualizes the challenge of creating antiracist school systems.

CHAPTER 3: COMMIT TO RACIAL EQUITY

In Chapter 3, we examine what it means to fully commit to racial equity—and how that commitment will suffuse an organization. By placing racial equity at the center of a school system, educational leaders extend the promise of public education beyond the circle of students and families that have historically benefited from it. The structures, pressures, and systems that continually regenerate and sustain inequity are often central features of schools and school systems—whether it is the social capital wielded by parents of influence or an accountability structure that forces teachers to triage reading interventions. Committing to racial equity means recognizing those patterns and reversing them.

CHAPTER 4: DISMANTLING TRACKING AND WITHIN-SCHOOL SEGREGATION

Chapter 4 turns the analysis to tracking and the curricular and aspirational objectives that school systems hold for their students. The chapter tackles the question of how to de-track a school system. The central task in de-tracking is to move teachers and curricula away from fixed notions of student ability and achievement and to reinforce rigorously to teachers and staff the primacy of a growth orientation to student achievement.

CHAPTER 5: MAKING SCHOOL DISCIPLINE DIFFERENT FROM POLICING

Chapter 5 shows how school disciplinary systems connect to broader patterns of policing and incarceration in the United

States. We need to ensure that teachers, particularly White teachers, have the cultural competence to engage BIPOC students in their classrooms. Additionally, school systems need to adopt restorative practices that seek to repair the injury to the school community when a disciplinary infraction occurs. The continued use of prevailing disciplinary procedures will only grow the school to prison pipeline and stifle the educational aspirations of students of color, particularly African American boys, who are grossly overrepresented in detention, juvenile court, and the prison system.

CHAPTER 6: IMPLEMENT STRATEGIC THINKING AND STRATEGIC PLANNING

Chapter 6 engages the need for strategic thinking and strategic planning as one undertakes the task of building an antiracist school system. Through strategic thinking and planning, you can identify potential allies and coconspirators who will be willing to support your work and join your courageous efforts as well defuse or ameliorate the objections of others. The point of this chapter is to clarify that building an antiracist school system doesn't just happen; it requires a strategy to achieve objectives and it requires planning to weave those objectives into a coordinated effort that institutionalizes the commitment you've made to students and to the community.

CHAPTER 7: CHOOSE GOOD TROUBLE: BE A BOLD AND COURAGEOUS ANTIRACIST SCHOOL LEADER

Chapter 7 ties these concrete actions together by showing the importance of courage and boldness in leadership. Committing a school or a school system to an antiracist agenda means that leaders must eschew timidity or an acceptance of the status quo. Tackling racial inequities, academic disparities, and historical oppression will likely be one of the most emotionally, physically, and spiritually draining endeavors of your career. You must also possess self-efficacy and believe that you can be a part of the change for the nation. Overcoming adversity will require you to be unapologetic about no longer accepting the status quo within public education—especially when it comes to BIPOC children.

CHAPTER 8: CONCLUSION

Chapter 8 concludes the book with some resources for causing Good Trouble and reemphasizes the need to recommit schools and broader society to the notions of equity and the value of activist leadership. Our hope is to engender school and community leaders who have the skills, dispositions, and knowledge needed to build antiracist school systems so that the values of equity and equality will persist and thrive in schools across the United States. The time to act is now.

Reflective Questions for Getting Into Good Trouble

1. **Personal Reflections**

   - To what extent has your personal history and cultural background shaped and influenced your reactions to race and equity?
   - What do you consider your strengths and challenges in leading for equity?

2. **Organizational Insights**

   - What are the major challenges and issues related to racial equity within your current school or school system?

3. **Initial Steps**

   - What are two to three initial steps or actions you can implement to address these issues?

4. **Long-Range Possibilities**

   - What action do you believe would most likely ensure that BIPOC students experience long-term success in your school?
   - What will your system look like if explicit bias, implicit bias, and systemic racism no longer impact student and staff performance?

5. **Anticipated Barriers and Challenges**

   - How will you involve the voices and experiences of key stakeholders (e.g., students, staff, parents, board members, community) in this process?

CHAPTER 2

Know Your History to Rewrite Your Future

GUIDING PRINCIPLES

1. Antiracist school leaders do the hard work of unpacking cultural, social, and historical narratives to discover uncomfortable truths about themselves and the communities they serve.

2. Antiracist school leaders promote research into the historical attendance patterns in their school system, understand the historical patterns of influence among privileged parents and constituents, and expose enduring patterns of inequitable resource allocation within and across the schools in their community.

3. Antiracist school leaders cultivate and encourage the expression of counter-narratives in order to delegitimize racist and non-egalitarian practices and to capture the vision of the social transformations they wish to see.

4. Antiracist school leaders strive to change established routines and social structures in order to dismantle the inequities that those routines perpetuate.

THE STORIES WE TELL—AND DON'T TELL—ABOUT OURSELVES

Everyone loves a story. Whether funny, sad, scary, or tear-jerkers, stories permeate our lives. They are how a child first learns, and stories help adults make sense of our experiences, our celebrations, our triumphs, and our defeats. Stories—and their close cousin, histories—anchor us within a social narrative in a way that connects us to others and to our past and to our possible futures. The stories and histories we tell about ourselves, our communities, our schools, and our students are not simply self-evident accounts of what has happened in the past. They are also justifications and rationalizations of how things became the way they are—or how things ought to be. This rationalizing part of storytelling—the moral of the story—connects the episodes of a community and a life into a coherent truth, a truth that should be more broadly known and understood. Stories tell us who we are and what we should become.

But not all stories are equal and not all histories are told. And not all stories are told to uplift and inspire. Within every group or community, there are the commonly accepted versions of history, preserved in yearbooks and newspapers, told in sermons, and recounted at city council meetings. These conventional stories we tell about our communities and their pasts define our understanding of ourselves and explain our lives to those outside the community. Sometimes, these community narratives of past events are told on a broader stage; when a tragedy strikes or when a local hero hits it big in Hollywood or in the National Football League (NFL), the local version of history is pushed out to the world. But all too often these conventional stories leave out more than important details—sometimes they omit entire swaths of people and experiences. The conventional tales and histories that form the accepted narrative of who-is-who and what-is-what do not always have room for people and events that are uncomfortable or inconvenient to some. And sometimes the powers that be do not want to remember events in ways that are outside the official versions.

In this chapter, we want to talk about histories and stories and the ways that finding, surfacing, telling, and showcasing these personal accounts of lives and power can help us understand and rethink the work that needs to be done in schools. By finding and sharing stories that have been suppressed or ignored or denied, you can begin to shape public awareness and public perception about students and parents whose educational needs have been neglected for far too long. As John Dewey wrote, "The past is a great resource for the imagination; it adds a new dimension to life, but on condition that it be seen as the past of the present, and not as another and disconnected world" (Dewey, 1923). The task of Chapter 2 is to show how schools can make the stories of a racist past, "the past of the present"—both connected to and a part of the worlds we live in. Learning, knowing, and telling your history is empowering and enlightening, and it is the first step toward equity.

The first part of the chapter lays out the power of storytelling and how stories provide frames for public policies and actions in schools. Essential for our task is the notion of "counter-narratives"—stories that unsettle the conventional narrative and highlight the experiences and voices of those who have not been included in official histories and official ceremonies. Counter-narratives help surface both the experiences of inequity in schools and the mechanisms by which inequity is produced and maintained. By finding, recounting, and telling counter-narratives, you will have a clearer way to present both the origins and consequences of inequity within your school or school system.

Finally, this chapter concludes with the recognition that knowing your history is not simply a pleasant trip through family photo albums or dusting off the old newspaper clippings. Knowing, telling, and ensuring that the history of all members of the community and all students is told and taught requires the decentering of traditional and conventional accounts. It moves offstage the concerns of some people and moves onstage the concerns of others. That move, simple as it may be, is provocative to some people and will, inevitably, prompt a pushback. In the final section of this chapter, we provide tips and tactics to engage that pushback and to ensure that the full story and history of students and communities of color are represented within schools. But let's begin with a story.

THE POWER OF STORIES: ALEXANDRIA'S TALES OF SEGREGATION

Thomas Chambliss Williams was in something of a box. As someone who believed, fervently, in the value and importance of racial segregation, he had fought long and hard against enrolling Black and White students in the same schools. Now, in 1959, in the wake of losing a lawsuit that fourteen Black students had filed to desegregate Alexandria's schools, the judge had informed the school district that school assignments could be based on "racially non-discriminatory" criteria—such as academic needs of the students or their maturity. This gave Williams and the school board an opening. They could use nonracial terms and categories to achieve their goal of racial segregation. Previously, the school system had simply assigned all Black students to the two Black schools, but the federal court now barred race as an official category by which to assign students to school, so the segregationists had to get creative. Williams was up to the task. He and the school board devised six criteria for evaluating whether these students could be allowed to enroll in all-White schools.

Not surprisingly, the "racially non-discriminatory" criteria barred all fourteen Black children from enrolling. Despite their impersonal quality, the words of exclusion had a sting: For example, Superintendent Williams wrote that the admission of one Black sixth grade girl, whose test score was above the median score of the White school to which she was applying, "would be a novel and unusual situation" that would be "a disruption of established social and psychological relations between pupils in our schools. . . . The situation would be an unnatural one," not contributing to the "normal and natural progress" for her or the other pupils (Reed, 2014, 37). In Williams's view, the novelty of a Black girl who scored higher than White students her age being in class alongside them, made the whole situation untenable. As he stated it, she was not being denied admission to the White school because she was Black but because the White students would have difficulty with the psychological implications of being taught next to a Black student who would, in all likelihood, outshine them.

And so it went for all fourteen students. Without mentioning the race of the students, the school district found all fourteen Black students unsuited for transfer to a White school. But race was fundamentally the only thing that mattered. Despite the district's efforts, however, Federal District Court Judge Albert V. Bryan ruled that nine of the fourteen students must be admitted to all-White schools. As a result, those nine students desegregated Alexandria City Public Schools on February 10, 1959.

But even after that momentous day, Williams and the school board continued to prevent Black students from transferring to the previously all-White schools. Their rejections of student transfer requests—couched in the racially "non-discriminatory" language required by the courts—still reeked of racial prejudice. A seventh-grade boy did not have "either the ambition or the spirit to enable him to compete successfully with even the lowest of the seventh grade" at the White school. Another student would be "hopelessly outclassed" by the White students in the sixth grade. The transfer of another Black student would only burden "the grade at [the White school] with more problems, which tends to slow down the whole grade." And so on. Each time the school board rejected a Black transfer request, the lawyers would seek and obtain a court order requiring that the school board approve the transfer. Not until September 8, 1960—18 months after losing their court decision—did the school board approve a Black transfer request without being subject to a court order.

STORIES CONNECT THE PAST TO THE PRESENT

This history in Alexandria is, like many civil rights histories throughout the South, simultaneously both well known and hidden. We all hear about *Brown v. Board of Education,* but we rarely hear about the deep resistance to school desegregation and integration that dragged on for decades across the United States—and continues today. Moreover, we don't see the connection between overt racist segregation and "natural" grouping and tracking based on student "ambition" or "drive." The histories of segregation and desegregation are well documented in hundreds, if not thousands, of academic books and personal memoirs. These accounts tell a rich and vivid story of systematic exclusion and denial of BIPOC students from a quality education. Other accounts tell of the dedicated and talented Black educators who, despite the constraints of unequal resources and lousy facilities, inspired generations of Black children. Yet, the fact remains that systemic injustices have plagued US education for decades upon decades, denying BIPOC students the quality education that White children and their families have grown to expect and demand from public school systems.

Despite the prevalence of these histories, the vast majority of White parents and families feel that those inequities of the past are unconnected to the inequities of today. The end of formally segregated education, they believe, renders any remaining inequalities as "natural," or the product of individual merit or failings. The point of this chapter is to show that this belief is both mistaken and holds enormous consequences for our present-day efforts to create equitable educational systems. The decisions and actions that limited the education of BIPOC students have a continuing resonance in contemporary schooling. These inequitable policies and practices laid down a foundation of behaviors, expectations, norms, and institutions that continue to deny quality education to BIPOC students. In order to determine how to move forward, school systems need to understand how their past made them what they are today. And it is the stories of people— students, parents, and teachers—within those school systems that connect policies to the lived experiences of communities.

STORIES AS WINDOWS ON POWER

In her book *Ghosts in the Schoolyard,* on school closings in Chicago, sociologist and poet Eve Ewing recounts the power of stories to explain more than just who did what to whom or to show one's proximity to injustice. As she tells it, stories are a way of knowing and showing; in fact, they are a kind of episte-mology: the "experiential knowledge of people of color not only is a legitimate source of evidence but is in fact critical to under-standing the function of racism as a fundamental American social structure" (Ewing, 2018, 7).

Let's break down Ewing's point a bit. She is saying that the expe-riences of people of color—who are typically left out of policy discussions—are perfectly fine sources of evidence on which to base public policy. That is, when we are debating whether to close schools in some neighborhoods, it is just as valid to examine how parents and students experience schools and the role those schools play in the community, as it is to examine test scores. Maybe even more valid. But she is also saying that those experiences do more than inform us about policy options; they are integral to understanding how racism is fundamental to the structure of American society. By telling—and letting us hear—the stories of school closure in the Bronzeville section of Chicago, Ewing enables us to see the intrinsic racism at work in Chicago schools.

Ewing's masterful book shows us that the histories and stories that emerge from the experiences of people of color are often counter to the official narratives that are frequently told to justify policies or practices. In Chicago, the official line was that the schools scheduled to be closed were "under-utilized and under-resourced." Ewing's digging into the stories of Bronzeville parents, teachers, and students showed that "under-utilization" was the result of racist housing and school segregation, and that "under-resourced" schools were the product of a school funding mechanism that robbed students of support when they stayed in their neighborhood schools rather than attend charter schools. The histories and stories of Bronzeville neighborhood schools showed that the failings in Chicago were the product of elite decisions to build a racist and unequal school system, but the community itself was being punished for those failings.

Richard Delgado writes that the status of stories is linked to the status of the storyteller. Outgroups, who lack power and influence, tell stories that are different from the stories told by the dominant group: "The stories or narratives told by the ingroup remind it of its identity in relation to outgroups, and provide it with a form of shared reality in which its own supe-rior position is seen as natural" (Delgado, 1989). That "natural-ness" of the ingroup's superior position is exactly what the fight for educational equity is aimed at. Fighting for equity means challenging the "normalcy" of stories traditionally told, unset-tling the narrative of why the existing distribution of resources is necessary or natural. These counter-narratives disrupt the conventional narrative, positing new heroes and new villains as we seek to disconnect the discourse from the flow of resources. As Delgado puts it, "Counterstories, which challenge the received wisdom, . . . can open new windows into reality, showing us that there are possibilities for life other than the ones we live" (Delgado, 1989).

In so doing, we not only imagine new possibilities but also uncover the means by which power is used to hide the reality of oppression. Conventional stories, told by ingroups, have a hard time even seeing the experiences of outgroups, and it is precisely ingroups' inability to see and know the experiences of outgroups that sustains and maintains inequities. As Milner Ball writes, "Blindness to people may be of a piece with their oppression" (Ball, 1990, p. 1856). The value of stories told by outgroups is that they reveal how inequity is both built and maintained. The marginalization of some students, the determination that their needs are less important, relies on discounting the stories that they, and their families, tell.

> Fighting for equity means challenging the "normalcy" of stories traditionally told, unsettling the narrative of why the existing distribution of resources is necessary or natural.

STORYTELLING AND THE FIGHT FOR EQUITY

So, the first step in building a movement for equity is simple: tell stories of inequity. While these stories often do not make it into official histories, they can be found if you ask the right people. Start by engaging those who experienced inequity: oral histories of former students and teachers, newspaper accounts of school closings, recollections at alumni gatherings, student-led research trips into the community archives, accounts of student–counselor interactions, remembrances of school suspensions and discipline practices—all of these are rich material that can provide counter-narratives to the conventional narrative of schools as sites of opportunity. In our experience, the fight for fairness in schooling has a long, vibrant—and often unrecorded and unrecognized—history. Particularly in places where news media or local newspapers no longer cover the local beat, the memories of past practices can shed light on how current practices evolved. While many parts of the United States have changed dramatically over the past fifty to sixty years, the continuities between past and present are often staggering when we consider how little has changed in the distribution of educational opportunity.

Another goal of counter-narratives—beyond connecting past practices to present conditions—is to honor the experiences of those who resisted inequity in the moment. These everyday acts of holding American society to its founding commitments might have been small protests or modest acts of resistance, but they preserved a tradition of Good Trouble that is, thankfully, a deep part of American culture and history. The democratic practice of making Good Trouble has many forebears and by telling their stories and sharing their visions of fundamental fairness, we honor their achievements. We also preserve and entrench the expectations that schools are the expression of a community's values, not the values of those who seek to hoard resources and build enclaves of privilege for only a select few. By telling stories and demanding action, we are not just advocating for those who have been robbed of an education. We are advocating for a system of governance that sustains our collective well-being.

WHAT KIND OF STORIES NEED TO BE TOLD?

Where do you begin? What parts of your school or community's history need to be told to understand and address the equity challenges before you? Sometimes the most straightforward stories can be the most illuminating: Who are the students at this school—and why these students? Do your school's demographics look like the demographics of the neighborhood? The school system? The community at large? The metropolitan region? If not, why not? What are the current school boundaries and how have those changed over time? If they haven't changed, has the population within the boundaries changed? What has caused that change? Has new construction of highways or housing divided the neighborhood or community? Have charter schools entered the community? Where have new neighborhood schools been built and how were those sites selected? We can ask a similar set of questions about class and poverty and how students in some parts of town are concentrated in high-poverty schools.

All of these questions aim to get at the composition of schools and how race and class play a role in who attends which school. Schools in the United States now experience more Black–White segregation than they did in 1968, the year Martin Luther King, Jr. was assassinated. At the same time, US schools have become more multiracial and multiethnic, with increasing numbers of Latinx and Black students attending school and more Asian American students attending schools with White students.

Activity: Tell the untold story of your school in the school newsletter or in a student-run podcast

2

Consider addressing some or all of the following questions.

- Who are the students in your school?
- Do your students reflect the demographics of the neighborhood? Why or why not?
- What is the history behind the drawing of your school boundaries? How were they drawn? How have the boundaries changed over time? Why?
- How have the demographics within those school boundaries changed over time? What are the reasons behind those changes?
- Who are the important decision-makers in the community? Do they reflect the demographics of the students in your school? Why or why not?
- List some local laws that have had an impact on the changing (or consistent) demographics of your school.
- What are the funding sources that support your school?
- Do your parent–teacher association (PTA) members accurately reflect the demographics of the student body?
- Interview parents and grandparents who attended the school and ask them what tracking looked like back in their day.

See "Both Substance and Symbolism Matter" section in Chapter 7 for a detailed example of how Alexandria City High School students shared the history of their school in public forums.

Overall, White students are the most racially isolated. The point is that these patterns do not emerge "naturally." They are the product of informal and formal decisions made by policy-makers, businesses, and individuals. But they have important consequences for the equity and quality of schooling that students receive.

The demographics of schools often drive the level of resources available to those schools and the responsiveness of school and school system leaders to the requests and demands of students and parents. What resources exist at your school that do not exist elsewhere—and vice versa? Where do these resources come from? Is there an active PTA raising funds to hire enrichment teachers or fund after-school programs? What sources of funding does the PTA rely upon? What kind of social and political capital do parents at this school have? Do they work with other highly influential people or do they have limited time and opportunity because of work obligations to attend PTA events? How do parents get on the PTA board in the first place? How does parent access to school and school system leaders affect the opportunities and resources available to their children?

Often these demographic and resource factors also drive larger policy issues that create even greater inequity in educational opportunity. What does the distribution of AP and Honors courses look like across schools? Or even within schools, which students find themselves in Honors pathways or AP World History? At what level do "talented and gifted" (TAG) programs begin? In middle school? In third grade? In first grade? How does enrollment in TAG affect future opportunities to take higher level courses in middle and high school? Ask parents or even grandparents who attended this school what tracking looked like back in their day. Do the racial disparities in AP course-taking look a lot like formal tracking of yesterday? Schools—and institutions more generally—often maintain policies because the cost of revising them (both political and economic) is not worth the payoff to the leader of the school or school system. Maintaining dysfunctional or inequitable systems because of the high political or economic cost of changing is known in policy circles as "path dependence."

Even if a school leader, as an individual, is committed to equity, they will be fundamentally unable to alter these practices if path dependence imposes significant costs on them for doing so. The point of counter-narratives is to change this calculus. This is done first by raising the moral cost of inaction by tracing the current inequity back to its origins, and, secondly, by imposing greater costs if school leaders *do not* alter those routines and practices. That is what making Good Trouble at school is really all about. Locating the source of inequity and then, through mobilization, imposing too great a cost on school systems if they fail to remove that source of inequity.

> Counter-narratives raise the moral cost of inaction by tracing inequity back to its origins and by imposing greater costs if school leaders do not alter those routines and practices.

BACKLASH AGAINST COUNTER-NARRATIVES AND CRITICAL RACE THEORY

Placing BIPOC actors at the center of these narratives is unsettling to many Whites. It challenges their worldviews and asks them to directly understand and confront the way that racism and racial discrimination have been at the heart of the American experience. White resistance to this broader, more systemic view of racism and White insistence on seeing race through an individualized lens, in which White "success" and BIPOC "failure" is the result of individual effort only, lie at the heart of racial conservative efforts to deny educators the opportunity to teach the facts and truth about race, racism, and the outcomes of systemic racism in the United States.

This effort to suppress critical race theory (CRT) took off in September 2020 when President Donald Trump, at the urging of conservatives opposed to the 1619 Project (a series of *New York Times* articles conceived and introduced by the *Times* journalist Nikole Hannah-Jones), banned all federal agencies from participating or providing any cultural competency or racial sensitivity training (including the Pulitzer Prize–winning 1619 Project and anything associated with CRT). On September 17, 2020, at the White House Conference on American History in the National Archives Museum in Washington, D.C., Donald Trump proclaimed, "Students in our universities are inundated with critical race theory. This is a Marxist doctrine holding that America is a wicked and racist nation, that even young children are complicit in oppression, and that our entire society must be radically transformed . . . critical race theory is being forced into our children's schools, it's being imposed into workplace trainings, and it's being deployed to rip apart friends, neighbors and families" (Trump, 2020). Unfortunately, this narrative posed by the former president has further entrenched racial division in the United States and has perpetuated the ideology that discussing the truth about racism is a threat to American democracy.

As you undertake the challenge of uncovering and telling the counter-narratives of your community, your schools, and your school system, remember that truth-telling is the first step in the fight for equity. Understanding our history is key to dismantling systemic racism in our schools. If opponents of your work claim that you are simply dredging up ancient history or reigniting racial discord, you might ask them what is it that they find frightening in the effort to tell true stories of the past and present? If we are to understand our present situation, we must understand how it connects to our past. The recent attacks launched against CRT are an effort to prevent the telling of those stories that connect the past to our current contexts and current dilemmas.

At base, CRT is an incisive framework for understanding how race and racism are not simply attributes of individuals but are woven into the fabric of our nation. It illuminates how racism, as a structural feature, is embodied in laws, policies, and practices that continue to oppress the most marginalized populations in the United States including Black, Indigenous, and People of Color. CRT has recently come into the spotlight, but it has long been used by writers and scholars to understand the experience and meaning and power of race in the United States—from the origins of slavery, through the Jim Crow era and the civil rights movement, to today's inequities in policing, housing, and schooling, among other domains.

> Critical race theory is not an ideology or a political movement. It is an intellectual framework that examines how race functions to distribute power within institutions and society.

CRT is not an ideology or a political movement. It is an intellectual framework that examines how race functions to distribute power within institutions and society. The origins of CRT date to the 1980s, when a group of legal scholars met at a workshop held at the St. Benedict Center in Madison, Wisconsin. Derrick Bell, Kimberlé Crenshaw, Richard Delgado, Jean Stefancic, Mari Matsuda, and Patricia Williams, among others, met to discuss how critical legal studies (which emerged in the 1960s and 1970s) could be applied to race and racial contexts in the United States.

Though these renowned scholars may have coined the phrase critical race theory, many prominent Black civil rights leaders such as W. E. B. DuBois, Dr. Martin Luther King, Jr., Malcolm X, and Shirley Chisholm spoke out against systemic racism in the United States and employed a critical analysis to advance the cause of civil rights and equity in the United States. A critical stance toward race simply means questioning and challenging existing racial contexts and racial norms in US history. Counter-narratives and counter-histories are simply another way of asking how our current notions of race and current experiences racism are tied to past practices—even though those practices (like chattel slavery and Jim Crow laws) have ended.

Most students in US school systems have not learned the accurate and horrific history of race in our country, in particular how the invented categories of race were (and are) used to advance and entrench White supremacy and oppress Black, Indigenous, and People of Color in the United States. They have not learned that the creation and use of racial categories as a mechanism of oppression have a legacy that lives on in ways that may not be readily understood or obvious. By using a critical analysis of systemic racism, you can pull back the historical curtain within your own local community and show the ties between the past and the present. Knowing your history is essential—in part so that you will not repeat it, but also so you can develop your strategy for dismantling systemic racism in schools.

CONCLUSION

On Wednesday, January 6, 2021, when we were roughly one-third of the way through the writing of this book, supporters of Donald J. Trump amassed on The Ellipse, just south of the White House, to hear President Trump and others repeat the unwarranted and unfounded claims that Joe Biden's victory was illegitimate, the election had been stolen from "them," and the only recourse was to violently disrupt the ceremonial counting of Electoral College votes. The crowd, stirred to "fight back," turned from the Ellipse and marched a little over a mile to the Capitol, where they proceeded to fight through bike rack barricades and a thin line of Capitol Police.

Many of the police at the Capitol resisted the surge, but others waved the virtually all-White crowd of rioters through, smiling and joking with them as they physically occupied the Capitol. The rioters interrupted the counting of Electoral College votes, killing a police officer along the way, and vandalized and trashed the People's House. Waving Confederate flags, some sporting Neo-Nazi clothing, the crowd was both thuggish and celebratory, exuberant and chilling. Some participants seemed caught up in the moment, others seemed to have steeled themselves for a violent and deadly encounter with the police and elected officials. In doing so, the rioters wound up causing the deaths of four of their own supporters.

Whatever the faults of American democracy, this unprecedented frontal assault on the machinery of presidential succession marks a deadly turn in both the cause of democratic self-governance and the backlash of White supremacists, who see the preeminence of White male control of American society slipping away from them. Their efforts to suppress not only the election of Joe Biden but also Kamala Harris, the first vice president of African American and South Asian descent, reveal the deep connections between racism and efforts to suppress democracy. White mobs have killed before in US history to prevent democratic self-governance from taking root and they have been especially active when Black voters threaten to undo the institutions and mechanisms of White supremacy. Today is no different.

To build antiracist institutions, to build antiracist schools, is to build a better and truer and more vibrant democracy. We can no longer ignore the persistence and power of White supremacy within our nation's politics and our institutions. If we are to rebuild our democracy, our only hope lies in ensuring that it is deeply and thoroughly antiracist. That means many elements of what has previously passed as acceptable or normal or how things are done must change. Antiracism is democratic work and democratic rebuilding requires us to commit to antiracist practices and institutions. The insurrection at the Capitol has revealed both who we have been and who we are; our task now is to recognize that a living democracy, fundamentally, requires a commitment to antiracism. We wrote this book as one small step toward building that commitment and that democratic life. Telling the counter-narratives of your community and your schools is your first step along this path.

Tips for Knowing Your History to Rewrite Your Future

2

- Ask members of your community who have experienced inequity to tell you their stories.

- Set aside the time to record one or two oral histories from former students and teachers. Ask them to share stories about student–counselor interactions, remembrances of school suspensions, and their experience of discipline practices.

- During alumni gatherings, plan on interviewing one or two alumni to ask them about their K–12 experience.

- Motivate your students to engage in student-led research trips into the community archives. Ask them to find stories of students protesting inequities and fighting for justice—finding examples of students engaging in the democratic practice of making Good Trouble.

Reflective Questions for Knowing Your History to Rewrite Your Future

1. **Personal Reflections**

   - What are the narratives that guide and inform your understanding of your own life and personal history?
   - To what extent have you developed counternarratives to those stories as you have matured and developed as a human being?

2. **Organizational Insights**

   - As you reflect upon your current school system or learning organization, what are the dominant narratives that are retold and perpetuated within its culture?
   - How do these narratives routinize and normalize the distribution of opportunity available to students?
   - To what extent do these narratives require counter-narratives to expose the truth of their origins and purpose?

CHAPTER 3

Commit to Racial Equity

GUIDING PRINCIPLES

1. Antiracist school leaders work to redress the racial inequities that have been affecting BIPOC students since their first days of schooling and which have been compounding over time.

2. Antiracist school leaders know that the failure to redress these racial inequities will result in lifelong financial, health, and well-being differences between White and BIPOC students.

3. Antiracist school leaders know that their job is to challenge the predominant paradigms in schooling and to better understand the contexts and circumstances of all children's lives.

4. Antiracist school leaders understand that their commitment to racial equity must be accompanied by a growth in racial literacy and racial fluency among all stakeholders within schools.

5. Antiracist school leaders are committed to personal transformation with the knowledge that such transformation will be unsettling. They fight against the deep resistance that may come when centering racial equity as the foundation of educational excellence.

This chapter has two goals: (1) to help you explain to your allies and coconspirators why racial equity is the central project of schools in our times and inspire them to take action and (2) to help you win over (or at least disarm) those who insist that racial equity is a secondary or even tertiary concern for school districts. In order to achieve these two objectives, we will make four arguments, which you can also use to promote greater racial equity.

1. Racism threatens more than the education of BIPOC children; it threatens their very existence.
2. Racial equity lies at the heart of any definition of excellence in schooling.
3. The actions of individuals matter deeply.
4. White perspectives on racial equity are, at day's end, different from BIPOC perspectives on racial equity.

WHAT DOES COMMITTING TO RACIAL EQUITY LOOK LIKE?

Some moments in time are, as we experience them, truly life-altering. We feel the potential and reality of change immediately, as it happens. In these moments, there is no turning back; we cannot undo or unsee or unknow the change that has transpired. The murder of George Floyd on the evening of May 25, 2020, and the summer of protests that ensued was one of those episodes in history in which a moment transformed a lifetime, galvanized a generation, and sparked a course of activism that continues to blaze. Other moments take on significance, only in retrospect—as we see how the course of events unfold in their wake. The connecting of dots, the drawing of an arc, the bend of a trajectory all enable us to see how far we have moved from our initial starting points, no matter where those points of origin begin. For many people, committing to equity happens because a crystalline moment of clarity convinces them, in a flash, that no other course of action is possible. Their understanding of the world shifts, permanently and irrevocably, and sets them on a path far different than their former course. For others, the commitment to equity is a steady recognition of necessary steps and an erosion of arguments that stand in the path of equity. It comes not all at once, but *poco a poco*, as the harm, pain and fundamental injustice of our society and schooling become too clear to ignore.

WHERE ARE YOU ON THE SPECTRUM OF COMMITMENT TO ANTIRACISM?

1. You have always understood the corrosive effects of racism and you have committed your career to advocating for, teaching, guiding, mentoring, and championing BIPOC students.

2. In a crystalline moment of clarity, your understanding of the world shifted, and you realized that no other course of action was possible.

3. Over time, you came to accept the consistent evidence of systemic racism and its detrimental effects on society and you came to understand that the arguments against its existence have ceased to make sense.

4. You are unpersuaded that systemic racism is the cause of racial, ethnic, and linguistic inequity.

A third set of actors need no such conversion. In particular, BIPOC educators have long both experienced those inequities themselves and committed their careers to advocating for, teaching, guiding, mentoring, and championing BIPOC students. BIPOC educators often establish deep and powerful connections with students who look like them and who come from the communities where these educators grew up within and live. Those connections of identity and geography, as well as the community bonds forged through those connections, do much to inspire youth and spark their passions.

This chapter is about how these three groups—lifelong equity advocates, converts to the cause, and those on the pathway to justice in schooling—can and should engage with a fourth group: those who are unpersuaded by the cause of racial, ethnic, and linguistic equity. There will be conflicts and lack of trust among the converted and those long committed to the cause—and both will be frustrated by the baby steps taken by those just now noticing the drip-drip-drip of denied opportunities to BIPOC students. But the challenge for those looking to get into Good Trouble at schools is to marshal those three groups within a school system and rally them to ensure that the fourth (Group 4) cannot stymie or thwart the steps necessary to put racial equity at the center of a school division.

Sometimes that will mean outreach and persuasion; other times, it will mean a more confrontational approach. Whatever the strategy, the challenge is to overcome the inertia, the whataboutism, and the efforts to deflect and deny the urgency of the current situation. Some members of Group 4 are overt racists. Others have, in the words of economists, a different "preference structure," which denies the centrality of race to the distribution of educational opportunity in the United

States. These folks, most likely, want to continue to deny that centrality for a host of reasons: their own privileges and opportunities, White fragility, and an ideological need to not see race. And among marginalized communities, fear or intimidation may have created a powerful instinct for self-preservation that resigns them to making no demands and simply accepting whatever the majority doles out.

In other words, Group 4 can be complicated. But your task is to ensure that these arguments are disentangled, dismantled, and defeated. Drawing on your stories within your communities, your next task is to ensure that the commitment to racial equity is as broad and deep as it can possibly be. Doing so will not only enrich the learning of BIPOC students but the learning of all students, indeed all members of the learning community: students, teachers, community members, parents, and school and district leaders, alike. Getting that commitment is essential to the systemic changes needed to fight systemic injustice and racism.

RACISM THREATENS THE EDUCATION—AND EXISTENCE —OF BIPOC STUDENTS

Sometimes the data speak for themselves and sometimes the data need a storyteller. When it comes to the experiences of BIPOC students within schools, the data show a stark, persistent, and meaningful difference between the educational outcomes of BIPOC students and White students. These differences—which we will document here—are useful to persuade some people about the necessity of grounding schools in the quest for equity. But the cause of these differences is the most important piece here: Schools expose White and BIPOC students to different curricula, different expectations, and to different school experiences. Decisions by school officials—teachers, principals, school board members, superintendents—set BIPOC students, in general, on an entirely different life trajectory than White students. For many of your stakeholders, just understanding the dynamics of this process will be enough to convince them that racial equity should be the primary focus of schooling.

Let's start at the beginning. We know that White students and BIPOC students enter kindergarten with different experiences and, on average, different levels of school readiness. Many of those differences, however, are due to disparities in household income and wealth between White and non-White households.

In fact, Roland Fryer and Steven Levitt were able to explain the Black–White gap in test results for a sample of 20,000 kindergarteners by taking into account seven factors: (1) a composite measure of the family's socioeconomic status, (2) the child's gender, (3) child's age at the time of enrollment in kindergarten, (4) family's WIC (women, infants, and children) participation (a nutrition program aimed at low-income mothers and children), (5) mother's age at first birth, (6) birth weight, and (7) the number of children's books in the home.

When Fryer and Levitt plugged those considerations into an analysis of student test scores, race was no longer a significant predictor. Controlling for these seven factors, they found that race was not relevant to the children's level of school readiness. What alarmed Fryer and Levitt, however, is that *over the first years of schooling, race became an increasingly accurate predictor of a child's test scores* (Fryer & Levitt, 2004). In other words, the longer a Black child stayed in school the bigger the gap between their White peers. And this loss is cumulative: in a follow-up study, Fryer and Levitt found that "On average, Black students are losing 10 standard deviations per year relative to Whites in the first four years of school" (Fryer & Levitt, 2006, 251).

This research suggests that the differences in test results for White and Black students *are school created*. Despite Fryer and Levitt's ability to statistically account for a racial difference at the beginning of school, they see a growing difference over time that they cannot explain without reference to race. In short, race becomes more and more salient to the educational outcomes of children the longer they stay in school. Based on this research, it's reasonable to conclude that, on average, schools *create* the test score gap between White and non-White students. The students stay the same, but their treatment by teachers and schools changes over time.

> Race becomes more and more salient to the educational outcomes of children the longer they stay in school.... Schools create the test score gap between White and non-White students.

The following statistics become even more haunting when we think about what those students experienced that generated these disparities:

- In 2019, White boys in fourth-grade public schools had an average reading score nearly three grade levels above the average reading score for Black boys (NAEP, 2019).

- In 2019, the percentage of fourth-grade White boys reading at an advanced or proficient level in public schools was 270 percent larger than that of Black boys. The percentage of fourth-grade Black boys reading at the lowest level was 210 percent larger than that of White boys (NAEP, 2019).

These disparities are not only relevant to grade school report cards; they have lifelong consequences.

- In a study of the Chicago school system, roughly 55 percent of third graders reading below grade level did not graduate from high school (Lesnick et al., 2010).
- In a nationwide sample, the percentage of students with the lowest reading scores in third grade accounted for roughly one-third of all students, but they accounted for nearly two-thirds of students who do not graduate from high school (Hernandez, 2011).

The brutal logic of unequal opportunities in school can be summarized as follows: despite entering school systems with mostly class-based differences in school readiness, the educational effects of an unequal distribution of wealth and income among students is, over time, racialized in schools, meaning that race accounts for a growing percentage of the differences in academic performance of BIPOC students compared to White students. If those differences are not addressed by eighth grade, students are assigned to less demanding course offerings and to inferior teachers. As a result, they experience enormous frustration upon entry to high school. This, in turn, produces further disparities at both ends of the educational spectrum: racially disparate rates of dropping out of high school and racially disparate rates of taking sufficiently demanding college preparatory courses that are needed to prepare for success in college.

Those outcomes are reflected in these following statistics:

- 11 percent of White ninth graders do not graduate high school within four years; for Black students, that figure is 21 percent (Table 3.46, Digest of Educational Statistics, 2018).
- Although Black students comprise roughly 15 percent of national enrollment in public schools in the United States, they represent only 6.4 percent of AP test takers (Kolluri, 2018).
- A 2010 College Board report found that Black and Latinx students enrolled in AP courses at half of the rate of White students (Wilson et al., 2014).

These AP credits don't just reduce the cost of college by awarding college credit for high school courses. They also increase the likelihood of college completion. One of the more robust predictors of graduating from college is the number of college credits a student has by the end of the first year after high school graduation (Adelman, 2006).

Students who have earned fewer than twenty units of college credit within that first year see their chances of graduating from college drop by one-third. Importantly, it doesn't matter whether those credits are earned before or after high school graduation. Twenty credits on a student's transcript—no matter whether the source is AP credit, dual enrollment credit, or traditional college credit—significantly increase the student's chances of graduation by over 30 percent (Adelman, 2006). That's why AP credits—and racial disparities in earning AP credit—matter.

They also, ultimately, translate into differences in income:

- A male student who drops out of high school earns only 47 percent of what a male college graduate earns; for women, that figure is 44 percent. A male student who doesn't complete college earns roughly 61 percent of the earnings of a male college graduate (Table E, Digest of Educational Statistics, 2018).

- Over the course of a lifetime, the differences between dropping out, graduating from high school, and graduating from college are staggering: the Social Security Administration tallied the difference in lifetime earnings between those not completing high school and graduating from college and found that male college graduates earned $1.3 million more than men who did not finish high school (Office of Retirement Policy, 2015).

These wealth and educational disparities directly translate into differences in health outcomes and life expectancy: an article published in the *Journal of the American Medical Association* in 2016 found that the richest 1 percent of men in the United States lived, on average, 14.6 years longer than the poorest 1 percent of men. But even when the income disparities were smaller, there were large differences in life expectancy: men at the 80th percentile of income in the United States lived six-and-a-half years longer than men at the 20 percentile of income (Chetty, et al., 2016). David Cutler, one of the study's authors, stated in an interview that the difference in life expectancy between these two groups is roughly five times greater than the change in life expectancy that would occur if scientists cured cancer (Ruell, 2016).

The chains of inequity are forged in the first four years of formal schooling and then wrap around kids during the next eight. Some modifications take place during the college years, but by then the pattern is basically set. In short, the causal chain is as follows: the differences in reading ability between White boys and Black boys at the end of third grade translates directly to eighth-grade academic performance, which translates directly to both dropout rates and course rigor in high school, which translates into AP course-taking which, connects to college completion rates, which connects to income, which yields markedly different life expectancies.

RACIAL EQUITY LIES AT THE HEART OF EXCELLENCE IN SCHOOLING

These statistics illustrate the inability of school systems to address the needs of BIPOC students. The growing salience of race to educational performance over time suggests that the experiences of BIPOC students within schools are different from the experiences of White students. Those differences, while perhaps initially small and subtle, are cumulative over time and have deep and enduring impact on the opportunities and performance of BIPOC students, compared to White students.

It is here, in the growing salience of race over a child's performance in school over time, that we see the effects of systemic racism at work. Decisions about which courses students should take (or want to take) in middle school and high school have their roots in the reading and math performance of students in fourth and fifth grade, which in turn emerge from teachers' successes—or failures—to build sound literacy and numeracy foundations by the end of third grade, a key turning point in the educational fortunes of students.

When each of those links is examined separately, race may have little to do with the pedagogical or placement decisions, but collectively they encode a pattern of educational expectation and performance that over time yields wide gulfs in opportunities for students. The interconnected chain of a teacher's emotional connection with a student, the student's exposure to rich and engaging materials, the students' mastery of fundamental skills, their performance in class and the teacher's recommendation for placement all string together. For some students, typically those who are White and affluent, that can be a string of pearls; for others, typically students of color, each nugget is like a lead weight, weighing down their fortunes and futures.

It is important to realize the systemic—as opposed to the individualized—nature of this process. On initial examination, decisions later in the cycle of the racialization of educational performance may appear to have little to do with race, but often they are the culmination of hundreds of earlier decisions about a teacher's assessment of student enthusiasm, which texts to assign, the formation of reading groups, and even sincere or patronizing encouragement. Institutional rules about performance and tracking that may appear "neutral" in seventh grade are in fact based on decisions that have been imposed upon those students from kindergarten to sixth grade.

That's why racial equity needs to be at the center of any definition of educational excellence. Connecting with children in the earliest years of their learning requires understanding who they are, where they come from, their interests, and their life stories. Cultural and racial differences within communities and across schools means that teachers working in these contexts must be culturally and racially literate and aware. It's not enough for teachers to "love all children." Teachers must have the skills, awareness, and insights needed to prevent their own decisions and actions from starting that process of racializing the educational opportunity debt. In short, teachers, particularly White teachers, need to be both racial literate and racially fluent. *Racial literacy* is defined here as a clear understanding of racial history and racial experiences of their students and colleagues (both BIPOC and White) and *racial fluency* is defined as a skilled ability to explain and navigate racial concepts and constructs related to education in the United States, particularly with students and families.

The challenge here is immense: nearly 80 percent of the public school teaching force in the United States is White, non-Hispanic while less than 7 percent identifies as Black, non-Hispanic (US Department of Education, 2021). The student body that they are teaching is majority students of color, with White students comprising 47 percent of all students enrolled in public schools. BIPOC students constitute 53 percent of public school students (US Department of Education, 2021). Given the fact that the demographics of the US teaching force and the K–12 population will not change rapidly over the next few years, it is imperative that White teachers, particularly at the elementary level, develop the racial literacy and fluency to connect with BIPOC students.

The use of culturally responsive and culturally sustaining pedagogies are key strategies to ensure that teachers have the skills, dispositions, and knowledge base to connect with students across racial and ethnic lines. Central to culturally responsive teaching is the recognition that a student's culture—including their community, history, heritage, and language—forms a rich source of connection and personal

> It is important to realize the systemic—as opposed to the individualized—nature of this process... Institutional rules about performance and tracking that may appear "neutral" in seventh grade are in fact based on decisions that have been imposed upon those students from kindergarten to sixth grade.

strength that, in the hands of a skillful teacher, can promote deep learning. Culturally responsive and culturally sustaining pedagogies are an expansive and burgeoning area of research. We cannot do full justice to the field in this chapter, but we want to highlight some important elements and how they connect to Chapter 2's focus on the transformative potential of counter-narratives. (For additional information on culturally responsive pedagogy, see the Appendix.)

Culturally responsive teaching, as described by Zaretta Hammond (2014), is premised on the capacity of teachers to foster a sense of trust with their students. That trust, and the reciprocal relationship that it produces, does more than just make a child feel good about school, their classroom, and learning. It creates the neurological prerequisites for independent learning and higher-level thinking. The causal chain is as follows: the brain is hard-wired to avoid threats and seek out community, for protection. Without feeling safe and valued within a classroom, a child, neurologically, has a harder time seeking connection with others since the brain's instinct for self-preservation is on high alert, producing stress levels that are incompatible with learning because they lead to higher levels of cortisol (essential to the flight or fight response) and lower levels of oxytocin (which promotes social bonding). Conversely, if a teacher can build positive social relationships with a child, they will induce within a child's "brain a sense of physical, psychological and social safety so that learning is possible" (Hammond, 2014, p. 45).

Once that baseline level of trust is established, "the teacher can provide a degree of 'push' or challenge without having the student experience an 'amygdala hijack' and either withdraw or become defensive" (Hammond, 2014, p. 75). Through core practices of affirmation and validation, teachers can build rapport with students that makes higher order challenges possible, inspiring students to take learning risks in a climate of trust. For Hammond, the key to those practices of affirmation and validation is listening to students and developing a deep understanding of the cultural contexts of their neighborhoods and households.

In a similar way, Luis Moll, Norma González, and their colleagues found that teachers who utilize the "funds of knowledge" that already exist within their students' households "will know the child as a whole person, not merely as a student, taking into account or having knowledge of the multiple spheres of activity within which the child is enmeshed" (González et al., 2006). By incorporating an understanding of the flexible and reciprocal networks of knowledge within and among households into their classroom pedagogy, teachers see their students' communities and existing modes of learning and knowledge as assets to leverage in the development of academic learning skills, rather than practices that hold students back.

Whether anchored in a neurological perspective that stresses the connections between learning and brain development or in a more anthropological or sociological perspective that focuses on capacities that exist within households and communities, culturally sustaining and relevant pedagogies move the task of teaching away from deficit framing that sees students and their families as deficient or inadequate. This cannot be stressed enough: deficit approaches that define BIPOC students as inadequate or lacking attributes necessary for academic and social success contribute profoundly to the racialization of academic failure. In contrast, culturally sustaining and responsive pedagogies make race and the racial expression of culture the foundation of educational excellence. In doing so, these approaches hold up the culture and dynamics of communities as sources of connection to and validation of students' lives and identities.

Undertaking this work, however, means that teachers and school leaders need to rethink their assumptions about race and education. In many ways, it means breaking the association in teachers' heads that White is the code for academic excellence. Understanding the cultural assumptions we make about students means seeing their communities and modes of cultural engagement as assets or keys to motivating academic success. This, in turn, requires teachers to evaluate their own racial self-understanding and the implicit (or explicit) biases they might hold.

And here we are at the nub: we all have biases. Every single one of us. Our brains are amazing in their remarkable ability to make associations even when we are not aware or conscious of those associations. The inclination and tendency to see patterns and extrapolate from patterns based on information at hand and messages from external sources is hard-wired into how our brains organize our world. The trouble is we are so good at making those associations that we do it without reflection: we associate highly visible characteristics like skin color with academic outcomes because the template for academic success that US society has presented to us is, in general, a White template. Our brains internalize that messaging in their relentless quest to be more efficient and to better understand the world. The problem is that process of internalization discounts other, less visible, explanations about what is going on with a particular child. Biases stem from our inclination to utilize these shortcuts without reflection. The answer to this dilemma is to slow down, to question our assumptions, and to question the frames of academic success presented to us. Culturally relevant and culturally sustaining pedagogies can help us reframe those terms of success and see the contexts of students' lives as resources through which to build connection and trust.

Doing so, however, challenges assumptions about Whiteness and the mostly unquestioned linkage between Whiteness and academic success. In Chapter 2, we discussed how counter-narratives can be used forge connections with and build an understanding of students' lives and to establish trust and reciprocity between educators and students. The same is true with culturally relevant and culturally sustaining pedagogies. Both, however, require skilled teachers, who understand the social contexts of students and communities in order to respond to the pedagogical needs of students.

In short, decentering implicitly White definitions of academic success means centering BIPOC experiences of academic success, but for a largely White teaching force to do so requires that they have a clear and deep sense of both racial literacy and racial fluency. Again, racial literacy is defined here as a clear understanding of racial history and racial experiences of their students and colleagues (both BIPOC and White) and racial fluency is defined as a skilled ability to explain and navigate racial concepts and constructs related to education in the United States.

> Decentering implicitly White definitions of academic success means centering BIPOC experiences of academic success, but for a largely White teaching force to do so requires that they have a clear and deep sense of both racial literacy and racial fluency.

Truth be told, many efforts to connect students to the past experiences of their BIPOC communities and their "unsung heroes" are all-too often patronizing and trite. Teachers without a firm grasp of the historical and socio-cultural contexts of segregation, formal and informal practices of discrimination, and outright assertions of power by White leaders often turn to empty celebrations of solo actors, without reference to the broader systemic dynamics of inequity, in which these achievements or acts of resistance took place. To be compelling and connect with the broader needs within the community, teachers need to understand how discourses about race have, in part, shaped and influenced their students' understanding of their own academic identities and to develop their own racial literacy and fluency. That is how and why racial equity is at the center of educational excellence.

THE ACTIONS OF INDIVIDUALS MATTER DEEPLY

As you come to understand how racism threatens the very existence of BIPOC students, it is important to not to become paralyzed by that knowledge. Too often the challenge that systemic racism presents becomes self-reinforcing, as the magnitude of the racism's impact overwhelms the sense of efficacy among those working to dismantle it. Committing to racial equity means recognizing the challenges but also recognizing the path forward. Uncovering and telling counter-narratives is a start, but challenging and confronting the forces that work against BIPOC students also require you to examine how (or if) antiracist work is undertaken within your school system.

Many school systems do not undertake antiracist work in order to advance equity. In our view that is a lost opportunity to put a halt, or least a brake, on the dynamics laid out in part one of this chapter. If we do not actively seek to reverse structural racism, the existing forces, institutional routines, and behavioral patterns will hold it in place. It takes affirmative steps to undo existing practices and place equity at the center of your school system. Our analysis of the racial opportunity debt and how it accumulates over time is aimed at motivating you and your team to undertake this work. But it's not easy work.

And we will be frank: this is work that White readers will need to engage more directly than BIPOC readers. Living in the United States as a Black or Indigenous person or as a person of color requires a sharp and keen understanding of how society and individuals define and enforce the color line. Whether that knowledge is telling young boys how to act in the presence of law enforcement to avoid being arrested or shot or is simply code-switching, the consequences and awareness of being non-White in the United States is ingrained at an early age. In contrast, many White readers of this book may not even think of themselves as having a racial identity, let alone understand how that racial identity enables them to move through the world differently than a Black student. In order to undertake the work of placing racial equity at the center of education, White educators, parents, students, and administrators must first engage their own racial views, racial literacy, and racial fluency in order to advance the project of building an antiracist school system.

A GROWTH MINDSET AND HUMILITY ARE CENTRAL TO ANTIRACIST WORK

Not all the members of your community—whether parents, school board members, or even staff—will be willing, initially, to undertake this self-assessment. Even BIPOC teachers or staff members may feel these issues are best left undisturbed. We advocate viewing these positions on equity as an initial starting point and recommend that you help your community adopt a growth mindset as you guide them through the complex challenges of putting equity first. That stance, that no one is fixed in their views, that no one is permanently, irrevocably, or irredeemably racist, is essential to your role as an educator. (It is also essential to the strategic thinking and strategic planning you'll undertake in Chapter 6.) In addition, humility about one's ability to understand across the racial divide is also a key component of success. This last admonition about humility is perhaps most aimed at White readers, if only because White actions have, in the past, been linked to worse outcomes for BIPOC students and communities. Doing antiracist work requires humility and a capacity to listen deeply to BIPOC staff, teachers, administrators, and community members.

FOUR STAGES OF INDIVIDUAL GROWTH AND COMMITMENT

Beyond maintaining a growth mindset and a sense of humility, we feel it is important to undertake a structured inquiry about how race works for the individuals within a community and within a school. This structured inquiry might be an individual or collective process, but we need to stress that it is a process—one that some members of your team may not complete or may resist completing. Building antiracist systems requires some attention to the racial views and skills of those participating in the construction of a new system. That individual level examination can surface surprising things; it can even be painful for some participants. And opponents of your work may seek to use the process to bring your work to a screeching halt. We stress that our discussion here assumes that the participants, while they perhaps vary in their willingness to undergo the process, are engaged as sincere participants. That may be a big assumption, but we have a hard time grasping how an antiracist school system could be constructed by staff and community members who are not at least willing to entertain the idea that racism affects the educational fortunes of students.

FIGURE 3.1 ● Stages of Self-Understanding for Antiracist Work

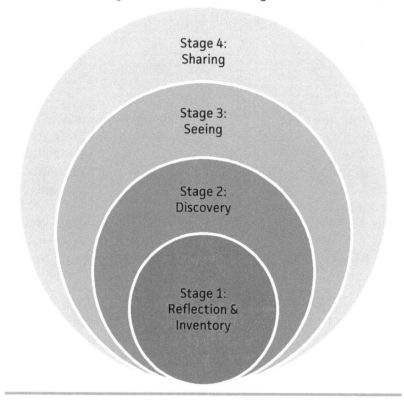

STAGE 1: REFLECTION AND INVENTORY

This inquiry begins by asking participants—whether they are teachers, community members, school board members, or whoever is listening—to evaluate where they are on a continuum of racial understanding and racial literacy. Figure 3.1 is a simplified schematic of this process of developing racial literacy and fluency. This process begins with a reflection on a person's own racial identity and an inventory of one's racial knowledge. How much do you know about the racial history of the United States and the broader world? Do you have an understanding of how race affects the lives of people within your community, particularly children in school? Do you ever talk about race? Do you ever talk about race with people who are not of your race? Why do you think that is? What has prevented you from engaging in this kind of conversation? Do you understand what a microaggression is and how it might affect students? The point of these questions is to connect each participant to the question of race in ways they may have not connected before. It's also the beginning of the process by which each participant comes to understand their own positionality within the effort to do antiracist work in schools. That deepening sense of positionality is central to each stage in this process, as it contributes to one's racial fluency.

STAGE 2: DISCOVERY

From this, the next step is to undertake a process of discovery, in which one builds up one's knowledge and reflects on one's own racial perspective, and one's own relationship to racism and what it might take to diminish the influence of racism within your community or school. At this stage, one is asking what would an antiracist stance look like in my life? Discovery can take many forms and it can take considerable time, depending on a number of factors, including the existing level of racial literacy and fluency within the school and/or community.

An important question to ask at this second stage is "Do I understand the difference between interpersonal racism and bigotry and institutional or systemic racism? In what ways do my actions—even if not individually racially antagonistic—contribute to systemically racist patterns in school? What is at stake for me in continuing—or abandoning—those actions? Why do I value or perpetuate processes or mechanisms that have disparate racial outcomes, even if they are facially racially neutral?" These questions delve into the purposes of administrative routines that sort and identify kids and asks participants to ask whether those purposes retain legitimacy in light of the racially disparate outcomes they generate.

Discovery can be a challenging and bumpy path, and it might very well elicit reactions of White indifference or White fragility, issues we will address below. Discovery is a fluid process, and for some White readers, it may be the most challenging stage through which to travel. Discovery—when undertaken with seriousness—forces one to evaluate sometimes competing values and to decide whether racial equity outweighs those other concerns. For leaders of this process, this may very well be the point at which there is the most pushback and resistance from the community, and it requires a strategic awareness of your goals and desired outcomes for your school, community, and school system. We will address those strategic implications in Chapter 6, but for now it is simply important to understand that discovery is a dynamic and challenging stage, made more complicated by the fact that different individuals are on different trajectories and different timetables in their discovery process.

STAGE 3: SEEING

In the third stage—Seeing—one further develops the capacity to see racism in action, in schools and outside of schools, and to understand how broader forces operate to sustain racism. This realm of seeing asks individuals to examine policies and practices in the community, in US society, even at the state or national level and examine whether they are linked, in important ways, to the operation of systemic racism within your school? Once you see those connections, if they are there, next ask yourself how might those connections be severed? How might the influence of both local and remote practices that sustain systemic racism be diminished? In short, the stage of Seeing seeks to generalize and apply the skills developed in the Discovery stage to a broader stage and across different institutions and actors.

STAGE 4: SHARING

In the final stage, Sharing, participants ask themselves whether they might share the knowledge and insights they have gained through the three other processes with others who are at the initial stages of inventory and self-reflection. This stage challenges participants to move from being an analyst to one who reaches out and undertakes conversations and actions to stimulate further change. Participants in Stage 4 come to view their own racial knowledge and literacy as an asset to an organization and have a clearer sense of how they might help others contribute to constructing an antiracist school system.

One key challenge in Stage 4 is, well, oversharing. For White participants in this process, we must stress that humility and careful listening are essential components of Sharing. We want to stress again for White participants that listening to BIPOC colleagues and understanding your own positionality (in respect to race, but also to gender, age, sexual orientation, and class) is central to being an effective communicator and constructor of an antiracist school system. There's nothing worse than a woke White guy telling Black or Latinx women teachers what to do. That's not getting us where we want or need to go. When done with respect and humility and while listening deeply, sharing can be a powerful means by which to build support for an antiracist school system. Without those values, we will not be successful in our efforts to rebuild schools.

THE CHALLENGES OF SELF-UNDERSTANDING

As teachers, staff, administrators, and school leaders pursue excellence by putting racial equity at the center of schooling, at least two challenges emerge. The first challenge stems from the willingness (or unwillingness) of various constituencies within a school or a community to engage questions of race, or to recognize that the disparities in educational outcomes are, at least in part, the product of how schools engage BIPOC students. Without a willingness to engage those issues, school leaders, district leaders, and teachers will be unable to locate racial equity at the center of educational excellence. The willingness to undertake this work stems from a personal and individual decision to engage. In the best-case scenario, the four-stage process outlined above will yield that willingness.

The second challenge stems from the issues that arise as that engagement unfolds. Everyone involved in this work acknowledges it can be messy and unclear and awkward and painful, full of contradictions and compromises. Our racial past as a nation is messy and painful, so how could forging a new racial future not be? But we do think there are steps you can take to facilitate that commitment to engage and to focus the activities of those involved on the important task of educating children.

Your first inclination may be to put people on a spectrum of racial literacy or competence: from antiracist at one end to overtly racist on the other end. That may be a useful tool to describe the positions of some folks, but we think the issue is more complex than that. In the United States, we have a long history of stifling conversations about race, therefore many White people adopt an initial stance about race that may be best described as discomfort, or a space in which they feel paralyzed by structural racism and the scale of the problem. If a White individual's discomfort is so great that it leads them to undermine or sabotage the conversation simply to avoid it, we can characterize that discomfort as White fragility (DiAngelo, 2018). Others may not demonstrate fragility but may instead be indifferent to racial disparities among students and divergent educational outcomes for White and BIPOC students.

THE TRIAD OF RACIAL DISCOMFORT, ANTIRACIST COMMITMENT, AND OVERT RACIAL HOSTILITY

Introducing the notion of racial discomfort (either in the form of indifference or fragility) to the equity spectrum provides, we believe, a more nuanced way to engage and lead conversations about race. As you develop strategies to engage your constituents and stakeholders, consider their initial starting point as a location in this three-sided field—a triangle mapped by antiracist commitment, racial discomfort, and overt racial hostility.

Figure 3.2 illustrates this and highlights the direction you need to pull your community in order to make progress on racial equity. You don't need all members of your community in the antiracist corner, but you need to map a region of supporters who are in the lower left-hand corner of Figure 3.2—in what we call a zone of transformation—in order to make progress. It's important to also realize that during your efforts to tug community members from a position of racial discomfort to antiracist commitment, they may very well slide closer to a stance of racial hostility, precisely because the push for equity may unsettle or disrupt their prior commitments.

In Chapter 6, we will return to this figure to discuss how to think and plan strategically about individuals and groups that

FIGURE 3.2 ● Mapping How a Community Moves From Racial Discomfort to Transformation

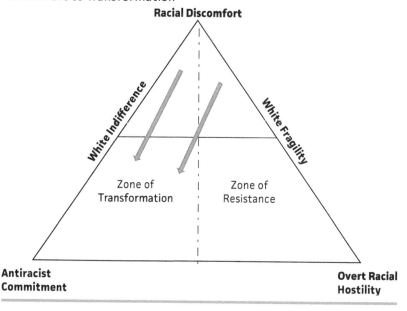

might want to pull your efforts to engage race into the lower right-hand side of that triangle. Because the line down the middle can be challenging to navigate, it is important to understand the probable reactions of those who seek to block your efforts.

Many BIPOC parents, educators, and administrators may be saying right now, "Why should we care about the feelings of White folks, many of whom have never given a damn about our feelings? Why do we need to walk on eggshells to avoid injuring the sensibilities of White people who don't like to feel bad about racism and the ways that they have benefitted from racism, whether directly or indirectly? In short, why should White fragility—the reluctance or inability to address issues of race without calling attention to the feelings of White people as they come to terms with race—derail the work of improving education for BIPOC students who have systematically received worse educations than White students?"

That is more than a fair question and one that we have tussled over and argued about ourselves. Ultimately, it is something of a strategic choice. In many communities, White people have the power to derail progress toward racial equity and that reality will require you to make a strategic decision about how best to proceed. We are unapologetic about identifying and naming sources of structural racism, but we also recognize that individual psychology means some people will seek to defend one's understanding of the world and one's place within the community, rather than changing their views. Unsettling or challenging preconceived notions of race is indeed threatening to some folks.

Greg's Story: Personal Challenges of Antiracist Work for Black School Leaders

Personally, as an African American leader, I did not realize how cruel, disrespectful, and unprofessional people in this world could be toward me until I began to lead our school system—unapologetically dismantling systemic racism during a global pandemic. It's ironic that trying to right wrongs brings great turmoil and distress. The moment that your school or school system becomes bold enough to expose your inequities, disparities, and systemic racism, you must be prepared to stand your ground and demonstrate resilience during the extreme pushback that you will face. I have been subject to outright threats and outrageous acts of disrespect including a time when a constituent expressed their hope that one of my loved ones would contract COVID and suffer from organ failure. I would have never thought that as a school superintendent I would have to move to an undisclosed area to prevent people from harming my family. This is not mentioned to deter you from doing this work; it's simply to prepare you for facing one of the biggest challenges in your career. You can't do this alone and must empower others to tackle these obstacles in collaboration with you throughout this journey to becoming an antiracist school or school division.

I still recall the first time that I was called [the n-word]. I was thirty years old before I heard a White person call me [n-word]. My wife and I built a new house in Hendersonville, Tennessee, where we were the first Black family in the new community. We were walking from our community pool with my father-in-law and our daughter, who was a toddler at the time. As we were walking home, a pickup truck with a Confederate flag flying sped down the street and a young White man stuck his head out of the window and screamed, "Go home you [N-WORD]!" I was numb and had so many thoughts go through my mind in a split second. It was surreal and then I was overcome with anger, sadness, confusion, and eventually rage from the fact that a White person had the audacity to say [the n-word], not only in my presence but to refer to me and my family as [n-word]s.

Though this was the first and only time so far in my life that I've been flat out called [the n-word] by a White person, I have consistently faced explicit and implicit microagressions, racism, bigotry, and various sorts of modern-day lynchings because of the color of my skin throughout my career and in my personal life. I recall on a community Zoom in 2021 someone put in the chat that I was a monkey, invoking the history of African Americans being likened to apes. Fortunately, I was not aware of this comment until after my presentation and our team was able to delete it from the public chat; however, the audacity to even post such a comment is unconscionable. But it is my reality. My work building an antiracist school system provoked this unjust treatment and it has exacerbated my racist experiences with some White people. You must be prepared to witness the worst in people and unfortunately you may even be threatened or attacked in the process.

BIPOC AND WHITE PERSPECTIVES ON RACIAL EQUITY ARE FREQUENTLY DIVERGENT

Our final claim in this chapter is a simple and frank admission: White perspectives on racial equity, at day's end, often diverge from BIPOC perspectives on racial equity—a challenge we've confronted ourselves as we've written this book. The individual experiences of our lives—inscribed with our intersecting and idiosyncratic identities—renders our views about what equity is, what it feels like, and what it takes to achieve it simply different. We stand in different places and see the world from those vantage points—whether as a Black woman, a Latinx trans woman, a straight White man, a Black man, an Asian American student identified with a disability, an unhoused emergent bilingual, or any of the infinite identities that exist among us. The point we hope to illustrate is that being aware of those differences in perspectives is essential to achieving racial equity. For White people, committing to racial equity means they must recognize those multiple perspectives and the power of positionality. It also requires an understanding of how school procedures and practices fail us by not recognizing and understanding that multiplicity of experiences.

CONCLUSION

There is a significant cost for not dismantling systemic racism in education. Our educational institutions play a key role in changing the narrative of the world because educators literally mold our next generations. Not addressing inequities will not only perpetuate the economic disparities in our country, it will also continue to perpetuate social unrest and division. Systemic racism impacts our economy by widening the wealth gap between people of color and their White counterparts. But intellectually recognizing the need for racial equity and taking the steps necessary to achieve it are two different things. This chapter has provided some guidelines to help you, your school communities, your stakeholders, and your constituencies commit to equity. That commitment will require significant introspection and personal growth and, as a leader, your task is to ensure that the processes of reflection, discovery, seeing, and sharing do not become derailed by distractions. The challenges are real, but centering racial equity provides a necessary foundation for academic excellence and a more just and democratic society.

Tips for Committing to Racial Equity

3

1. Take affirmative steps to identify and undo existing practices that harm BIPOC students and place equity at the center of your school system.

2. Become racially literate—develop a clear understanding of the racial history and racial experiences of your students.

3. Become racially fluent—develop the skills to explain and navigate racial concepts and constructs concerning the educational system in the United States and in your particular community.

4. Provide professional learning to enhance the racial literacy and racial fluency for all the teachers in your school.

5. Ensure that teachers are using culturally responsive and culturally sustaining pedagogies in the classroom.

6. Design a school community that celebrates the cultures and traditions of the students in your school. Nurture a school culture where children take pride in their ethnic backgrounds.

7. Consistently and explicitly challenge assumptions about Whiteness and decenter implicitly White definitions of academic success and instead center BIPOC experiences of academic success.

Reflective Questions for Making the Commitment to Racial Equity

1. **Personal Reflections**

   - How would you describe yourself as an advocate for equity?
   - How do you deal with individuals who are committed to maintaining the status quo—or seem defensive when engaged in crucial conversations about equity?

(Continued)

2. **Organizational Insights**

   - List the ways you agree or disagree that a commitment to antiracism in educational organizations is essential to the survival of our democracy.
   - If you were to estimate, how do the staff of your school or school system align with the four groups identified? How do the actions of the individual contribute to the functioning and culture of educational organizations?

3. **Initial Steps**

   - How are you working to identify the range of individual attitudes and perspectives evident among your staff, parents, and community? How can you determine how they divide into the four groups identified in this chapter?

4. **Long-Range Possibilities**

   - How can you organize professional learning to engage staff in honest and sustained discourse about the impact of inequity upon student achievement and well-being of BIPOC?

5. **Anticipated Barriers and Challenges**

   - What areas of resistance or challenges to open discourse about equity are most commonly expressed in your current school or school system?

CHAPTER 4

Dismantling Tracking and Within-School Segregation

GUIDING PRINCIPLES

1. Antiracist school leaders understand the potential for tracking systems to produce significant educational harms and work to produce equitable systems that provide an excellent educational experience to all students.

2. Antiracist school leaders work to ensure that no student is locked into a path that limits their options.

3. Antiracist school leaders are aware of how tracking, special education, and gifted and talent programs have been used to segregate students based on race and work to ensure a representational balance in all programs.

4. Antiracist school leaders work to ameliorate the damage done to students by tracking programs including student motivation, engagement, and achievement with lowered educational interest, attainment, and performance.

5. Antiracist school leaders train teachers to differentiate instruction, they incentivize rigorous course work, and they personalize learning to accommodate the unique strengths and to maximize the achievement of all learners.

Thurgood Marshall had reason to feel good—and optimistic. A few hours earlier on the morning of May 17, 1954, the US Supreme Court handed down the famous *Brown v. Board of Education* decision, banning formal racial segregation in Southern Jim Crow classrooms. Now, Marshall, the legal strategist and mastermind behind the Brown litigation effort, stood in a crowded hallway in a midtown office building that served as the headquarters of the National Association for the Advancement of Colored People (NAACP) in the New York City. Under the bright lights of television crews and as reporters jotted down quotes, Marshall stood alongside the association's leaders and luminaries—men like Walter White, the NAACP executive secretary; Channing H. Tobias, chair of the NAACP's board; Arthur B. Spingarn, head of the NAACP Legal Defense Fund (LDF); Ralph Bunche, political scientist and UN under-secretary general; and LDF assistant counsel Robert L. Carter.

Executive Secretary White took the occasion to announce that the NAACP would move beyond the schools issue and tackle residential segregation and job discrimination: "We will use the courts, legislation and public opinion to crack the iron curtain of segregation." Perhaps feeling the flush of a long-fought victory, Marshall made a prediction of how long segregation would last: he pronounced that it would take "up to five years" to eliminate segregation in education across the entire country, adding, in the words of a *New York Times* reporter "that, by the time the 100th anniversary of Emancipation Proclamation was observed in 1963, segregation in all its forms would have been eliminated from the nation" (N.A.A.C.P., 1954).

Unfortunately, Marshall's predictions were off—way off. Meaningful, wholesale integration did not take place in the South for another seventeen years, not until 1971 when the Supreme Court approved busing as a remedy for the constitutional violation of segregation. In some cities like Chicago, desegregation and integration never really took place at all. By the late 1970s, enthusiasm for school integration waned, within both Black and White communities, and the Supreme Court began crafting mechanisms for school systems to get out of court-ordered integration. By the early 1990s, earlier gains in promoting integration began to erode and now segregation is as bad in the United States as it was in 1968, when Martin Luther King, Jr. was assassinated.

In many ways, this book has become necessary because of the continuing inability of the school systems to generate equitable learning opportunities for students, either segregated or integrated. If Thurgood Marshall had been right on the day that *Brown* was decided, you would not be reading this book. Not only is segregation very much alive and well in US schools and society but new forms of segregation—particularly within-school segregation—mar the landscape of education in the

United States. In the wake of court-initiated desegregation and integration efforts, many schools resorted to more informal ways to maintain distance between White students and BIPOC students. At times, school leaders pursued these strategies to maintain the racial division among students. At other times, school leaders thought that this separation of students by course offering was in the best interests of all students. Either way, the segregation of students by course rigor is one of the key sources of educational inequality and inequity in the United States today.

Despite the belief by some educators that differentiated course offerings benefit all students, research has repeatedly shown that tracking or ability grouping of students is profoundly harmful to the educational interests and outcomes of students placed on the lower tracks and, simultaneously, provides little or no academic benefit to students on the upper tracks. Despite this strong research finding, many students, typically BIPOC and low-income, are unable to access the full curriculum offered by schools. This school-level choice to not provide equal access is a persistent and damning failure of US public schools.

This chapter explores the issue of tracking and within-school segregation. First, we highlight the major research findings that demonstrate its shortcomings as an educational strategy and next examine its racial implications for sorting students within schools. Second, we explore the political reasons why, despite the abundance of research, tracking and ability grouping hold such a tenacious grip, particularly within racially mixed schools. At base, tracking exists because of fundamentally divergent views on the objectives of schooling, ideas about student abilities and growth, and the prevalence of zero-sum thinking about student opportunities. Finally, we examine the results and strategies of communities that have de-tracked and what goes into a successful de-tracking campaign.

The goal of this chapter is to help you identify where and when tracking is occurring within schools, to marshal arguments against it, and to deploy strategies and arguments to minimize (hopefully eradicate) its pernicious effects. Because of its connection to "common sense" arguments about student achievement (arguments that do not hold up under scrutiny), tracking is a perennial, almost gravitational, policy within US public education. The battle against tracking is not won in a fell swoop but must be waged continuously. It requires teachers, parents, school administrators and district leaders to push back against the calls to sort students into two groups: those that receive demanding and creative instruction and those that do not.

In the previous chapter, we wrote about the data showing how inequitable the US educational system is. In this chapter, we want you to stay focused on data but a particular kind of data. Not data about where students wind up but data about what you offer them. Equity requires understanding how learning opportunities are distributed within your school system and ensuring that all students are provided comparable opportunities to learn (OTL). Tracking, by its very definition, abandons the notion that students should receive equitable opportunities to learn and instead seeks to sort and stratify students, exposing them to different levels of rigor, different content, and, ultimately, different life and career options. Data will be your ally as you seek to combat that differential treatment, but you will need to focus on a particular kind of data: input data, not output data.

> Tracking, by its very definition, abandons the notion that students should receive equitable opportunities to learn and instead seeks to sort and stratify students, exposing them to different levels of rigor, different content, and, ultimately, different life and career options.

Advocates of tracking will focus on output data—in particular, the differences in test score performance between students of color and White students (as well as between affluent and low-income students). They will use those differences in achievement data—and they are real—to justify exposing different students to different levels of content and rigor. But that "solution" is precisely what created those differences in the first place. Tracking magnifies and exacerbates differences in educational outcomes within the early stages of education and formalizes those into persistent, rigid, and confining educational trajectories. If the "achievement gap" (and, truth be told, we really don't like that term) is to be closed, it will be, in part, because tracking is not used to withhold rigorous academic content from one group of students. In fact, we see the existing disparities in test score outcomes more as a measure of the educational debt US schools owe to students who receive worse instruction and lower expectations. Fixing this—and addressing this debt—is an absolute imperative, but it's not easy.

WHAT EXPLAINS ACADEMIC ACHIEVEMENT?

Before we get into how tracking works, it's important to understand what drives the differences in learning outcomes that show up in the first years of schooling. While children learn a lot of things in the first three or four years of schooling—such as social skills, independence, initiative, persistence, adaptability, self-control, bodily control, community mindedness—schools often focus most on specific skills or curriculum mastery linked to statewide standards. Over the past twenty years (since the enactment of No Child Left Behind), the focus on test scores and meeting proficiency standards in math and English language arts beginning in third grade has been more or less unrelenting.

This standardization of testing has shown significant differences in scores for White students and for BIPOC students. Despite the pressures of accountability, this gap has not appreciably closed over the past twenty years. Accountability-based policies have mandated consequences (sometimes severe) for schools, teachers, and students if test targets are not met. Despite these sanctions and punishments, the differences in test score performance between White and BIPOC students, on a national basis, has remained more or less constant for a generation.

Take a look at Figure 4.1. The chart shows the percentage of students who hit the proficient or higher benchmark on the National Assessment of Educational Progress (NAEP) reading test from years 2005 to 2019, classified by grade level and race. While the percentage of Black students scoring proficient or higher increased over that time period, less than 20 percent of Black students were proficient in reading in fourth and eighth grades in 2019. Importantly, the percentage of White students who scored proficient was roughly 30 points higher throughout this time period. In fact, the gap never really closed at all.

FIGURE 4.1 ● Percentage of Students Proficient on NAEP Reading by Race and Grade, 2005–19

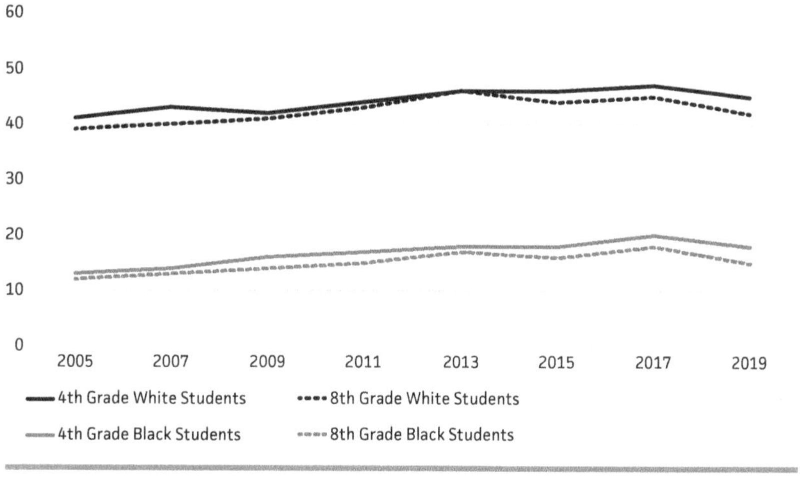

Source: The Nation's Report Card. Data Tools. NAEP Data Explorer.

https://www.nationsreportcard.gov/ndecore/landing

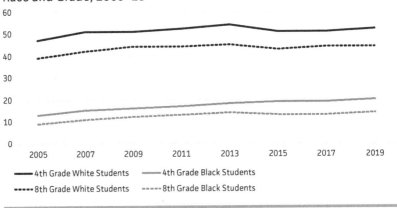

FIGURE 4.2 ● Percentage of Students Proficient in NAEP Math, by Race and Grade, 2005–19

——4th Grade White Students   ——4th Grade Black Students

•••••8th Grade White Students   -----8th Grade Black Students

Source: The Nation's Report Card. Data Tools. NAEP Data Explorer.

https://www.nationsreportcard.gov/ndecore/landing

Similarly, Figure 4.2 shows the NAEP math results: the gap stays very consistently at 30 percentage points between 2005 and 2019.

Many nonracial factors help account for these differences between White and Black students. In fact, one of the most powerful predictors of test scores is household income, with poverty strongly correlated with lower performance. Poverty not only creates stress and uncertainty within households but also contributes to poor nutrition, worse health care, and higher rates of mobility, all of which harm educational outcomes (Duncan & Murnane, 2011). Poverty, however, is not evenly distributed, with Black children experiencing poverty at a rate three times higher than White children (26.4 percent for Black children vs. 8.3 percent for White children) (Thomas & Fry, 2020). Another factor explaining the differences in proficiency rates for Black and White students is parental educational levels, which exert a strong influence on a child's readiness to learn, with higher levels of parental education associated with higher test scores for their children. While Black high school attainment has increased steadily over the past forty years, reaching near parity with the United States as a whole, Black college graduation is still significantly lower than the national average. In 2019, Black college attainment was only 73 percent of the national average (Day, 2020). With poverty and educational levels being two of the biggest drivers of test score performance, and given the uneven distribution of both poverty and education, the differences between Black and White children shown in Figures 4.1 and 4.2 become a bit clearer.

But they don't account for all the differences. To fully understand what is going on, we need to examine the social contexts of neighborhoods, communities, and schools. Children are affected by more than just their families and households. They are situated within schools and neighborhoods that exert additional effects on their well-being. When schools and neighborhoods see higher rates of poverty, outcomes are often worse for children than in more affluent neighborhoods, *even for children who themselves are not poor* (Reardon, 2016).

This is particularly true when racial segregation intersects with economic segregation at the school level. In short, we need to remember how both individual characteristics of households and group characteristics of neighborhoods, schools, and communities—and their relative degree of racial and economic isolation—directly influence student performance. The neighborhood or school effects can act as a kind of multiplier in the context of a family or household. Teasing out the relative contribution of those multiple sources can be exceptionally difficult, but the key point is to realize that the context of schools and communities often have an independent effect that goes beyond households and families—and the two interact.

FROM SEGREGATION TO TRACKING AND BACK TO SEGREGATION AGAIN

This interplay of test score performance and school and community context gives tracking its particularly cruel dynamic and circular logic. Students who are performing worse, because of their individual and community contexts, are exposed to less demanding work to facilitate their mastery of it. However, rather than promoting mastery and confidence, the assignment of less complex and challenging work to students on a lower track yields the opposite effect, with lower track students intensely aware that other students are presented with more challenging tasks. They also do not learn as much, both in terms of content and in terms of skills (Oakes, 2005).

When the BIPOC students on the lower track look around and see that most of their lower track peers are students of color and that the upper track students are more likely to be White, the association between race

When the BIPOC students on the lower track look around and see that most of their lower track peers are students of color and that the upper track students are more likely to be White, the association between race and academic achievement becomes fixed in their view.

and academic achievement becomes fixed in their view—with Whiteness signifying accomplishment and achievement and BIPOC students associated with lower performance and failure (Tyson, 2011; Legette, 2018). That—combined with simplistic, unchallenging, and rote material they are assigned—leads to less academic engagement, less curiosity, and less inclination to, fundamentally, care about school outcomes (Tyson, 2013). When you couple this with the systemic racism across the United States that cannot be avoided at this time, then our BIPOC children start their educational journey at a disadvantage. At the systems level, this dynamic produces a two-track system that fundamentally miseducates large swaths of students simply because the school system believes it's more efficient to teach homogenous clusters of students (Levin, 1990).

All of this starts at an early age. The identification of students as "talented and gifted" often begins in the early years of elementary school, and it typically starts within the mathematics sequences taught by schools. For example, the Gifted and Talented exam in New York City Public Schools was, until 2021, administered to four- and five-year-olds prior to the beginning of kindergarten, with the results of that one test determining whether a child would be offered a slot in the city's Gifted and Talented program (School Diversity Advisory Group, 2019, p. 29). Because of the sequential nature of math, and the need to transfer skills from earlier courses to subsequent ones, divergences in math experiences become the basis for much tracking. By late elementary, math groupings become increasingly rigid and upon the transition to middle school, they effectively formalize student assignment to an upper track or conventional (or lower) track. The biennial survey of middle school principals that accompanies the NAEP, revealed that, between 1990 and 2011, roughly 74 percent of all eighth graders were in tracked mathematics programs (Loveless, 2013, p. 17). Once on a particular track, a student will find it difficult to move to a higher track, particularly in math as a student's prior placement becomes the basis for the next placement.

The sixth or seventh grade math placement is key. Being assigned to pre-algebra in middle school effectively places students on a college track, as it aligns with a trajectory that has students completing Algebra I by eighth grade. Once students age out of self-contained classrooms and begin moving classrooms for each class period, higher level math placement frequently indirectly affects a student's placement in other courses. The payoff for this sequence (and continuing with a rigorous curriculum) is a much higher chance of completing college. According to a US Department of Education study of the effects of course-taking on educational outcomes, an African American student whose curriculum is in the top 40 percent of difficulty and who takes an additional math course beyond Algebra II increases their chance of attaining a college degree from 52 percent to 66 percent. For Latinx students, the chances jumped from 45 percent to 69 percent (Adelman, 2006, p. 92). Similarly, students who take courses with low expectations and low rigor have much higher rates of dropping out or not attending college. Indeed, one study found that students in the lower academic tracks are roughly 60 percent more likely to drop out of high school (Werblow et al., 2013).

These filtering mechanisms are stratified by race and by class. If we think of enrollment in Advanced Placement (AP) courses in high school as the end product of a long line of tracking decisions, we see the cumulative effects of that course-level segregation. In 2014, according to the College Board, Black students comprised only 2.8 percent of students taking the AP Calculus BC exam, widely regarded as the most demanding AP math exam, even though Black students represented 14.5 percent of all high school graduates that year. Latinx students represented just 7.3 percent of the AP Physics C: Electricity and Magnetism exam test-takers, even as they comprised nearly 19 percent of high school graduates (Kolluri, 2018).

Black students represented only 5.0 percent of AP European History test-takers and just 7.7 percent of US government examinees (Kolluri, 2018). (On the other hand, 65.6 percent of Latinx students took the AP Spanish language exam, but that is not clear evidence of steering students toward a demanding curriculum (Kolluri, 2018).) Estimates of the participation rate of low-income students show some recent improvement because of federal aid to pay for the tests, but one study (Theokas and Saaris, 2013) estimates that low-income students participate in AP exams at less than a third of the rate of middle- and high-income students—when their schools even offer the exam.

For students who are identified early as gifted or talented, there are social consequences as well as academic consequences. In general, identification of "talented and gifted" students is disproportionately skewed to White and upper-income students (Peters et al., 2019). For high achievers, this early designation does more than just expose them to more demanding and engaging material; it also changes their self-conception as learners and as individuals. Using a paired sample of "gifted" and "regular" students in Germany making the transition from grade school to middle school, Vogl and Preckel (2014) found that students assigned to the higher track expressed higher levels of social acceptance and interest in school, even though they had comparable test score performance as the students in the lower track.

The students in the lower track also experienced worsening relations with teachers over time. The authors conclude that "an intellectually challenging environment and being with equally able peers seem to be decisive factors for fostering social acceptance and a positive class atmosphere" (Vogl & Preckel, 2014, p. 63). The stratification of students leads to an internalization of social reward that boosts students' self-perception and sense of social standing and belonging. Placing some students in a clearly designated "smart group" provided a boost to their feelings of belonging, better connected them to the school, and improved (comparatively) their relations to teachers. It is important to note Vogl and Preckel did not account for race in their study, possibly because it was undertaken in German schools, which lacked measurable racial diversity. In the US context, failure to account for the racial dynamics of tracking would be unimaginable, given the racial disparities in assignment to higher and lower tracks. All of these factors, over time, will increase student performance, independent of the particular abilities of students.

We should also note the powerful effects of stereotype threat. The stereotype threat, in educational contexts, posits that Black or Latinx students are aware of the things people say about their racial identity and academic performance. That awareness, in turn, harms individual student performance because students understand that any time their performance falls short it will, in the eyes of others, confirm the stereotype. The stereotype lives in the world as a looming threat waiting for confirmation; the obligation to perform under the cloud of such a threat induces worse performance. So, rather than seeing your poor test performance as the result of a traumatic situation you experienced the night before or because you worked a late shift, others perceive your performance as tied to your race. As Claude Steele writes, "We know that anything we do that fits the stereotype could be taken as confirming it. And we know that, for that reason, we could be judged and treated accordingly" (Steele, 2010, p. 5). Or as Steele adds, Black students understand that "one false move could cause them to be reduced to that stereotype, to be seen and treated in terms of it" (Steele, 2010, p. 7).

The stereotype threat has been shown empirically to reduce test scores significantly, but it seems to be strongest in precisely those settings in which BIPOC people are rare and it seems to most affect those with the highest ability (Steele, 2010). In other words, given the existing low levels of BIPOC students in AP courses, those few who do find themselves (mostly isolated) in AP courses are most prone to the stereotype threat. That, in turn, leads some teachers and school counselors to conclude that many BIPOC students just "aren't ready" for the rigors of demanding coursework.

WHY DOES TRACKING PERSIST?

Given these effects of tracking on student ability to access the full curriculum, and the harmful effects it has on student learning, why does tracking still exist? What forces keep dividing students into two or three groups and then doling out challenges and learning in either meager or generous portions? The short answer: teachers and parents. The longer answer: school boards and school leaders who, while running complex organizations, fear alienating the two most powerful constituencies within schools—teachers and parents. The result is the maintenance of a system that simplifies the lives of teachers, parents, and administrators, but quite literally deprives many students, mostly BIPOC, of an education. Tracking helps the most powerful voices and harms the unheard voices—and that is why it is hard to eliminate. To begin undoing tracking, however, we have to understand the motivations of those who support it. Two different motivations animate teachers and parents, but they wind up in the same place. For teachers, tracking is a labor-saving device; for parents, tracking is an insurance policy (but one they don't really need).

Many (but not all) teachers hold the strong conviction that students learn best when they are clustered together by roughly comparable levels of skill or ability. A homogenous grouping, so the thinking goes, makes for easier and better learning than a heterogeneous grouping. It's easier to focus students' attention and to communicate with them about the skills and tasks at hand when they are, literally, all on the same page. To have students approach material with a range of backgrounds, a range of insights, and a range of connection to the material forces teachers to be creative, resourceful, and innovative, on a continuous basis. That is, quite frankly, exhausting for many. It's far simpler to present standard pedagogical chunks to cohorts of students who look at a problem or text with the same background knowledge, experience, and motivation. Just as an assembly line makes the manufacture of a car simpler by routinizing activities, tracking removes the need to customize instruction for the particular needs of a student.

In short, homogenous grouping exists not because it makes learning better but because schools, as organizations, seek to make teaching simpler.

The problem is that the assembly line approach to teaching is producing different kinds of cars for different students—or leaving out essential parts altogether. With tracking, not every student gets all the parts needed for a functional, smooth-running machine; some get Cadillacs or Mercedes-Benz, while others get go-karts, often without steering wheels. While having a diversity of student backgrounds, talents, inclinations, and motivations within a single classroom places more demands on teachers, it also ensures—when done well—that everyone has a reliable, dependable, and effective vehicle to get them to where they want to go.

For many parents, the problem is different: they like the fact that tracking will put their child on the path to success, even if others are left behind. For them, education is a competition, not a common or shared enterprise. This fundamentally boils down to a difference in worldviews: some parents are satisfied with an absolute level of quality within their children's schools, but for others the standard is relative. For the first group, as long as the schools are doing a good enough job with their child, meeting goals, and ensuring that essential skills and knowledge are conveyed and developed, they're satisfied.

For the second group, aka the competitors, schools must always be judged not in relationship to specific goals but relative to all other schools. These parents are satisfied only when the relative advantages of their children are greater than most—precisely because they see schooling as a competition in the struggle for status and resources. In short, tracking is an occasion for them to engage in opportunity hoarding. Typically well-off and well-educated, these parents contend that the important metrics for schools are not whether a child meets robust educational standards, has a healthy self-image, and a community-minded spirit but does the local high school produce Ivy League admission letters and National Merit Semi-Finalists?

Tracking, in their view, makes the latter outcomes far more likely. Many parents see the challenging work of attending to the divergent needs of learners within a heterogeneous classroom as reducing the amount of time a teacher spends with their child—and they're probably right. The reality, however, is that the students from upper income, well-educated households are, on average, going to thrive and succeed within public schools, and in college—whether tracking exists or not. Parents are, nonetheless, risk averse about their children's education, and rightfully so. You only get one opportunity at a K–12 education. Because there are no do-overs, many parents see tracking as necessary to minimize distractions in the classroom and to ensure that their child is surrounded by like-minded and talented students. These parents feel peer effects are more important than parental influence or a child's own motivations. The problem is the evidence just doesn't support this view.

In general, higher performing students, as measured by test scores, do not on average perform better when surrounded by other high-performing students (Gamoran, 2009). The benefits of tracking for high achievers are generally overrated by parents, and the harms of tracking for students in the lower track are vastly underestimated by teachers and administrators.

According to Gamoran (2009), tracking yields greater inequality without greater productivity. In other words, tracking maintains a system of inequitable access that provides little benefit to those at the top and much harm to those at the bottom.

> The benefits of tracking for high achievers are generally overrated by parents, and the harms of tracking for students in the lower track are vastly underestimated by teachers and administrators.

The challenge for administrators is that teachers and parents comprise two of the most influential constituencies within public education. Without the support of these groups, no school board member would survive reelection and few superintendents would see their contracts renewed. Organized and resourceful, these two groups have the capacity to make life very difficult for administrators who oppose them.

SO HOW DO WE DE-TRACK?

We want to be frank: de-tracking is hard to do and you can botch it up. A poorly de-tracked system will produce worse outcomes for all students. While it might seem like ripping off the band-aid is the best approach to de-tracking, that strategy has some clear adverse consequences for students who have not been adequately prepared for more demanding math, science, and English coursework and are suddenly confronted with rigor and acceleration. A successful de-tracking plan sets up children for success over the long haul and works systematically to reverse the effects of inequities that have compounded over time.

What follows is a set of guidelines and practices that will enable you to obtain the benefits of de-tracking and avoid the worst possible outcomes. Clearly, entire books can be (and have been) written on de-tracking and how best to accomplish it; what follows here is a set of general guidelines and moderately specific tasks as you undertake this work or advocate for it.

RESOURCES AND REFERENCES FOR DE-TRACKING

Ascher, Carol. (1992). "Successful detracking in middle and senior high schools." *Clearinghouse on Assessment and Evaluation*, ERIC Clearinghouse on Urban Education. ericae.net/edo/ED351426. htm.

This article examines the evidence that supports de-tracking, and proposes various components of successful de-tracking, influenced by scholars such as Anne Wheelock and Robert E. Slavin. Additionally, it includes suggestions of the author, such as alternative assessment methods and accelerated schools. Overall, the author argues that the key to successful tracking is inclusivity by providing lower-track students with the same resources and engaging educational experience as higher-track students.

Burris, Carol Corbett. (2015). *On the same track: How schools can join the twenty-first-century struggle against resegregation*. Beacon Press.

In this book, Burris speaks about her experiences as the principal of a high school and the successful methods they used to de-track that dramatically improved student outcomes and almost closed the achievement gap. These outcomes contradict the fears and misconceptions that de-tracking is harmful to high achieving students.

Burris, Carol Corbett, & Garrity, Delia T. (2008). *Detracking for excellence and equity*. Association for Supervision and Curriculum Development.

This book details the authors' experiences with de-tracking, examples of other schools' de-tracking processes, and strategies for beginning to de-track successfully. These suggestions include beginning with teachers who are interested, eliminating the lowest track first and affording parents and students the agency of making the decision for themselves.

Hyland, Nora E. (2006). "Detracking in the social studies: A path to a more democratic education?" *Theory Into Practice*, 45 (1): 64–71. www.jstor.org/stable/3497018.

This article looks at the pedagogical approaches recommended for teaching social studies and explains their similarities to those of de-tracking, such as democracy, inquiry, and civic participation.

Marsh, Richard S., & Raywid, Mary Anne. (1994). "How to make detracking work." *The Phi Delta Kappan*, 76 (4): 314–317. www.jstor.org/stable/20405324.

This article argues that to execute successful de-tracking, the entire system within a school must be restructured with careful planning, acknowledgment of concerns, adequate teacher preparation, and new practices to support it.

Rubin, Beth. (2006). "Tracking and detracking: Debates, evidence, and best practices for a heterogeneous world." *Theory Into Practice*, 45 (1): 4–14. 10.1207/s15430421tip4501_2.

This article covers the history of de-tracking, examples of different implementations, and strategies for the most effective ways to de-track.

Rubin, Beth C., & Noguera, Pedro A. (2004). "Tracking detracking: Sorting through the dilemmas and possibilities of detracking in practice." *Equity & Excellence in Education*, 37 (1): 92–101. https://doi.org/10.1080/10665680490422142.

The authors in this article reflect upon their experiences and the literature surrounding de-tracking and argue that successful methods of de-tracking must be comprehensive and holistic pursuits that incorporate the needs of marginalized students at the forefront.

Slavin, Robert E. (1990). *Cooperative learning: Theory, research and practice*. Prentice Hall.

This book details the approach of cooperative learning, one of the main strategies used in de-tracking, created by the author.

Slavin, Robert E., Welner, Kevin, & Burris, Carol Corbett. "Alternative approaches to the politics of detracking." *Theory Into Practice*, 45 (1): 90–99. doi: 10.1207/s15430421tip4501_12.

This article suggests two methods to implement de-tracking, which include winning the community over in schools where the community would be receptive to equity initiatives and trust the school to advocate for them and taking them on in schools where the community is resistant and refuses to incorporate equitable practices into their educational practices.

(Continued)

(Continued)

Welner, Kevin, & Oakes, Jeannie. (1996). "(Li)Ability grouping: The new susceptibility of school tracking systems to legal challenges." *Harvard Educational Review*, 66 (3): 451–471. https://doi.org/10.17763/haer.66.3.p92775298646n342.

These authors use case studies to argue that court mandates and educational researchers can be key in introducing de-tracking in schools that resist it.

Wheelock, Anne. (1993). *Crossing the tracks: How "untracking" can save America's schools*. The New Press.

This book explores six common characteristics of successful de-tracking in schools, and details specific experiences and issues tackled by various schools that have de-tracked.

Yonezawa, Susan, et al. (2002). "Choosing tracks: 'Freedom of choice' in detracking schools." *American Educational Research Journal*, 39 (1): 37–67. doi:10.3102/00028312039001037.

This article looks at racially mixed high schools to prove that the freedom of choice model, which allows parents and students to choose whether they want to de-track, leads to little progress for lower tracked students into higher tracked classes because of institutionalized barriers and attitudes surrounding minority students' abilities and aspirations.

De-Tracking Middle School and High School Math

Ithaca, New York, and San Francisco, California

Sometimes the challenge of de-tracking can appear overwhelming. The first question is "Where to start?" Many districts have answered that query by starting with middle school math. Some systems have, in effect, deregulated tracking, allowing students to select their preferred level of math course regardless of their test scores or teacher recommendations. Others have taken a more robust approach, intentionally grouping students in heterogeneous classrooms with a wide range of learning abilities, in effect creating a common math curriculum for all students.

The lessons from these districts can be summed up in three ways: start small, with initially modest changes and then gradually making more significant adjustments. Go deep, with a strong focus on building deep comprehension of math concepts in middle school, which can lay the foundation for greater success in high school. Finally, invest in teachers. Teaching across a wider array of math backgrounds requires a versatile skillset and may require smaller classes to enable students to engage in the hands-on application of concepts to tasks.

Ithaca City Schools (ICS) in Ithaca, New York, has embarked on de-tracking their math program at the middle and high school levels to ensure educational equity for their Black and Hispanic students. A study on their work in the Hechinger Report (October 2020) highlights their efforts to de-track their mathematics programming in middle school to change the outcomes for students in their high school mathematical experience.

According to the report, ICS formerly separated its middle school students into three math levels, producing pronounced racial segregation in math: the lowest math tier was 70 percent Black and Hispanic while only 25 percent of the entire middle school student population is Black and Hispanic.

Beyond the equity concerns, teachers also expressed frustration prior to de-tracking with the math skills of students who were accelerated into upper tracks. Many of them lacked a comprehensive grasp of math knowledge and, as a result, they performed poorly in advanced math courses in high school.

Ithaca's response was to start small: first, the district consolidated three math pathways in eighth grade into two and merged the two pathways in seventh and sixth grade into one. The school system hired additional teachers to provide smaller learning support groups and began engaging staff through professional learning.

Similarly, San Francisco Unified School District (SFUSD) began de-tracking its middle school and high school math curriculum in 2013. That program relied on the state's adoption of the Common Core State Standards to push all students toward higher math knowledge. By fusing its middle school math pathways into Common Core Math 6, Common Core Math 7, and Common Core Math 8, the system sought to deepen all students' understanding of math concepts. The district's signature approach was to develop conceptually rich courses that go deep into content and ask students to apply those concepts in concrete tasks.

(Continued)

The results have been impressive. The percentage of SFUSD students who failed Algebra 1 in ninth grade dropped from 40 percent of students to 8 percent, and fully a third of high school students went on to take the most rigorous pathway in later high school years, the highest in the history of the district. De-tracking produced lower levels of failure and a greater percentage of students pursuing advanced math.

Both Ithaca and San Francisco—two very different cities—saw significant parental pushback. In Ithaca, a member of a group opposing de-tracking went on to win a seat on the ICS school board. Both districts, however, have maintained their commitment to ensure all students have access to the full math curriculum.

CONCLUSION

The racial disparities in tracking are staggering but not surprising. Tracking emerged in US schools just at the time that desegregation and integration was forcing White and Black students to attend schools together. Tracking effectively denied Thurgood Marshall his victory by recreating on the classroom level what he fought so tenaciously against at the school level. Understanding the limitations of *Brown v. Board of Education*, as well as the linkages connecting within-school segregation and between-school segregation, is essential to fighting the equity fight.

As you develop your plan to combat tracking, be stealthy as you evaluate this tenacious foe. As you analyze your school or school system, think about the specific stakeholder groups in your community who will oppose your efforts to dismantle tracking. Most likely, the stakeholder group with the most opposition will be White families with influence and affluence. White privilege and White supremacy utilize tracking and ability grouping to maintain de facto segregation. It's not a coincidence that most talented and gifted programs, specialty, and many magnet programs and schools within schools (such as International Baccalaureate programs) are predominantly White. The connections between Jim Crow schooling and tracked curricula are clear, robust, and long lasting.

To help you engage those who will oppose you, fall back on the language of equity and equal opportunity under the law to support and buttress your work. Leaders like Thurgood Marshall understood the power of rhetoric to inspire and overcome, even as he realized the depths of racism within US society. De-tracking will hit a nerve, but by fighting this fight, you will be in a long line of fierce equity advocates who have made US schools better for all as they secured a quality education for their children.

Tips for De-Tracking Successfully

4

- *De-tracking is complex, and it takes time.* Tracking touches on multiple dimensions of a school system—from course scheduling to teacher recruitment and staffing to community engagement and outreach. De-tracking requires systemic change, a gradual and steady undoing of past practices that engendered systematic inequality. It is a marathon, not a sprint.

- *De-tracking requires a strengths-based approach.* De-tracking challenges conventional notions of academic success and excellence. To de-track successfully, school leaders need to shift away from deficit understandings of student skills and culture and more thoroughly understand the resources, talents and vibrancy of students, families, and their communities and see them as sources of knowledge and expertise.

- *Develop an opportunity to learn dashboard.* Develop and utilize an opportunity to learn (OTL) data system that identifies the resources and curricular offerings made available to students and evaluate whether those opportunities to learn are distributed equitably—by school, race, ethnicity, gender, language use, disability, national origin, religion. Identify where those disparities are most acute.

- *Come up with a strategic plan.* Develop a strategic plan for de-tracking that draws on the OTL data system to establish clear benchmarks, milestones, and metrics for what a de-tracked system looks like. This plan should both anticipate sources of opposition and advance a strategy for overcoming that opposition. This plan should also include fallbacks and second-best options if de-tracking strategies are not working.

(Continued)

(Continued)

- *Provide teachers with the professional learning they need to de-track successfully.* Commit to ensuring that teachers have sufficient resources and training to undertake new instructional tasks. De-tracking requires that teachers develop a broad array of strategies and skills to engage the full spectrum of student needs. To do so requires time and resources committed to professional learning.

- *Solicit help from local community leadership.* Focus teaching strategies on asset-based approaches that utilize a deep appreciation of the culture, community, folkways, and local leadership to foster deep learning, especially in elementary years.

- *Get buy-in from parents and community leaders.* Undertake outreach and community engagement with parents and community leaders to explain the existing inequities within the system and how tracking results in a de facto segregation within schools, particularly within high schools. Enlist parent and community support to keep a focus on the equity rationale for de-tracking. Develop teacher leadership—particularly within math and science—to help explain the issues at the school level and to parents.

- *Set high academic expectations for all students.* Commit to high standards and deep learning for all students, with a particular focus on middle school and early high school. While these may build off existing state standards, they may also exceed them. Link these standards to the OTL data system to ensure that students have sufficient resources to master the new challenges.

- *Begin providing students with the rigor they need at the elementary level.* Phase in the removal of tracks for math and science placements over several years beginning with elementary schools. This phase-in allows for teacher professional learning in middle and high school and ensures that students are not abruptly confronted with material they could not reasonably be expected to master. As an interim step, infuse lower-track courses at the middle school level with increasing expectations based on the OTL data system and newly adopted standards. By targeting those courses with the lowest cognitive load and academic expectations, and ratcheting up those expectations steadily, while simultaneously also phasing out tracks in the lower years, you will eventually bring both students and courses into alignment with higher expectations and performance requirements.

- *Make AP and honors level courses the default.* At the high school level, develop an opt-out rather than opt-in enrollment policy in honors and AP courses. That is, at specified junctures within the curriculum the expected and normal course sequence will be within honors courses and will culminate in an AP course in either eleventh or twelfth grade. Any student who does not wish to follow that sequence must obtain parental, teacher, and advisor approval to do so.

- *Structure for inclusion.* For those students who do exercise the opt-out policy, establish co-enrollment courses in which AP and non-AP students are instructed within the same course, taught by the same teacher at the same time. Allow full and free transfer back into the AP course if a student feels that they are confident enough to take the AP exam. Co-enrolled courses, in which both AP and non-AP students are taught side-by-side by the same teacher at the same time, enable a student to easily transfer into regular (or honors) biology, for example, without disrupting their course schedule or even informing their peers. For the overstressed and overtaxed student whose mental health is imperiled by the AP and International Baccalaureate (IB) academic arms race, co-enrollment courses can be a much needed safety net.

- *Use numbers to fight the stereotype effect.* Ensure that BIPOC students who are enrolled in AP or honors courses have a critical mass of fellow BIPOC students alongside them in these courses to send clear messages to teachers and to all students that AP and honors courses are not simply a White domain. Often, co-enrollment (see above) can provide that critical mass of peer support that aids BIPOC students.

Reflective Questions for Dismantling Tracking and Within-School Segregation

1. **Personal Reflections**

   - Does your current school system use ability grouping within elementary school classrooms? To what extent is your school system's use of ability grouping tantamount to tracking?

(Continued)

2. **Organizational Insights**

   - What do data (e.g., student achievement, test scores, enrollment in rigorous coursework, postgraduation success in education and career pathways) suggest about the impact of ability-level grouping or tracking in your school or school system?

3. **Initial Steps**

   - Based upon your analysis of student performance data, what are your top three to five priorities for equity related to the dismantling of tracking in your school system or school?
   - How can you and your staff collaborate to ensure that a rigorous, uniform curriculum enables all students to engage in challenging programs and courses?

4. **Long-Range Possibilities**

   - If you were to develop a project plan for a multiyear process for de-tracking, what would be your first-year priorities? What would you include in your second- and third-year plans? What are the long-range outcomes you hope to achieve by the end of a five-year cycle?

5. **Anticipated Barriers and Challenges**

   - How will you present a rationale for this process of de-tracking so that you get maximum buy-in from various individuals and stakeholder groups with vested interest in current policies and practices?
   - What are the major implications for professional learning as you lead staff toward a more equitable and less "leveled" approach to student grouping?

CHAPTER 5

Making School Discipline Different From Policing

GUIDING PRINCIPLES

1. Antiracist school leaders work with parents, students, teachers, and staff to create disciplinary processes that create community and restoration.

2. Antiracist school leaders build an educative and formative disciplinary structure that sees children as both responsive to their communities and adaptive to the needs of that school community.

3. Antiracist school leaders understand the nature of the school-to-prison pipeline and its racist impact on BIPOC students and take steps to disengage the school system from the juvenile justice system.

4. Antiracist school leaders challenge the use of zero tolerance policies within schools at every opportunity.

5. Antiracist school leaders look explicitly at the racial disparities in disciplinary actions and work to eradicate them.

6. Antiracist school leaders engage in culturally sustaining and restorative practices to establish the needed relationships and bonds with students required to build trust and mutual respect.

SCHOOLS AND STREETS

In his best-selling book *Between the World and Me*, Ta-Nehisi Coates talks about life as a teenager in West Baltimore and the violence that marked his experiences on the street and in school:

I came to see the streets and the schools as arms of the same beast. One enjoyed the official power of the state while the other enjoyed its implicit sanction. But fear and violence were the weaponry of both. Fail in the streets and the crews would catch you slipping and take your body. Fail in the schools and you would be suspended and sent back to those same streets, where they would take your body. And I began to see these two arms in relation—those who failed in the schools justified their destruction in the streets. The society could say, "He should have stayed in school," and then wash its hands of him (Coates, 2015, p. 23).

Coates's denunciation of schools as simply another system of violence designed to control the bodies of young Black men shocks the conscience of those who, as he puts it, believe in the Dream. The Dream posits the United States and its schools as sources of opportunity and support for young minds and bodies, as institutions that educate and train them, nourishing their curiosity and sustaining their well-being. Coates contends that schools present two options to young students of color: conformity to rigid and mindless discipline or being turned loose, abandoned, and left behind.

WHAT IS SCHOOL DISCIPLINE FOR?

Most principals, teachers, and superintendents—particularly those who work at schools attended by predominantly BIPOC students—might not recognize themselves in Coates's depiction of Baltimore schools. They might argue that they're simply trying to create a safe environment for the students who want to be at school and who want to get an education. To protect those students, they argue, sometimes requires a disciplinary structure that reinforces norms and standards of conduct in a vigorous way. To ensure a safe haven for the majority, those who violate the norms of the community must be dealt with. And in communities already surrounded by violence, so the logic goes, schools must enforce rules firmly to keep that violence at bay, to create a refuge for students who want to learn.

But the numbers tell a different story: BIPOC students are much more likely to be disciplined within school and much more likely to experience exclusionary disciplinary punishments (either out-of-school suspensions or expulsion) than White students. Even when analysts control for the socioeconomic status of students, Black students in particular experience more frequent punishments and harsher punishments. Moreover, when White and Black students commit the same offense, Black students receive harsher penalties. In short, the school to prison pipeline is not a metaphor; it is a reality for far too many students. Students who receive out-of-school suspensions are more likely to find themselves within the criminal justice system than students who do not receive them. Importantly, students with disabilities are suspended at significantly higher rates than the general school population.

Antiracist school leaders need to create disciplinary processes that create community and restoration, rather than separate, divide, control, and punish communities. They need to move their schools to an educative and formative, not punitive, disciplinary structure that sees children as both responsive to their communities and adaptive to the needs of that school community. Fundamentally, antiracist educators need to understand the nature of the school-to-prison pipeline, its racist impact on students who are BIPOC and take steps to disengage the school system from the juvenile justice system. Finally, school and district leaders need to construct, with students, a disciplinary system founded on restorative practices.

This chapter first examines the disproportionality that BIPOC students experience within the school disciplinary systems, exploring the way that race and gender shape their interactions with school officials. Next, the chapter looks at some of the causes of these disproportionate outcomes, focusing on both the emergence of zero tolerance policies and the racial mismatch of the teaching force and the student body within US schools. The chapter then turns to the connection of the school disciplinary system with the juvenile justice system and the "policification" of schooling over the past 30 years. Finally, the chapter examines alternative strategies for schools and the role that restorative practices can play to ensure that students receive fair and equitable treatment. This section also explores how school disciplinary systems can become more educative and formative process, rather than punitive.

RACIAL DISPARITIES IN SCHOOL DISCIPLINE

Think back on your high school years. Think about the things you did that make you wince a little now. Then think about the things you did that prompted someone to take notice and do something about. Now think about all the things you did that no one knew about—or at least no grown-ups knew about. Whether it was pulling fire alarms, roaming the school roof, or simply cutting class, we all have those memories, and they make for good stories at high school reunions and in wedding toasts. But for some students, those actions were not simply future reunion reminiscences. They were life-altering moments that diverted them from the school system into the juvenile justice system. And the pace of that diversion has been increasing for some time now. Maybe you were a goody-two-shoes or maybe you were just lucky, but if you went to high school in the 1980s or 1990s, your chances of getting expelled or suspended for your conduct were significantly lower—no matter what your conduct was. Indeed, over the past three decades now, the rate at which schools have been suspending or expelling students has nearly doubled, from 3.7 to 6.9 percent of students (Petras et al., 2011).

Utilizing the National Longitudinal Survey of Youth that interviewed some 9,000 students annually between 1997 and 2010, Shollenberger in 2015 found that nearly a third of all students in the United States experience an out-of-school suspension during their time in the K–12 system (Shollenberger, 2015). But those suspensions are not evenly distributed: Shollenberger's study found that over the course of their time in school, 67 percent of Black boys experienced out-of-school suspension. In a national sample of all districts with more than 3,000 students (encompassing 85 percent of all students in US public schools), the Office of Civil Rights for the US Department of Education found in 2012 that while African American students represented only 18 percent of students in the sample, they constituted 35 percent of the students who were suspended once, 46 percent of students suspended more than once, and 39 percent of all students who were expelled. In addition, the survey, the Civil Rights Data Collection, found that "Across all districts, African American students are over 3½ times more likely to be suspended or expelled than their White peers" (Office of Civil Rights, 2012).

In some major cities, the disparities in suspension rates are staggering. In Chicago, Black students make up 45 percent of the total enrollment but 76 percent of all suspended students. In Wake County, North Carolina, those numbers are 24 percent of enrolled students and 57 percent of suspensions. In Dade County, Florida, Black students comprise 25 percent of enrolled students and 50 percent of all suspensions. In fact, in the top twenty largest school districts in the nation, the *average* difference between the percentage of total enrollment who are Black and the percentage of suspended students who are Black is 22 percentage points (Office of Civil Rights, 2012, p. 4).

It is important to note that Latinx students, in general, have lower suspension rates than Black students. The Office of Civil Rights in the US Department of Education found little discrepancy between the percentage of Latinx students enrolled and the percentage of Latinx students suspended or expelled. The deep disparities in school discipline policies affect Black students much more sharply than other students of color and are clearly borne out in the literature (see Welsh & Little 2018 for an overview); the findings on Latinx students are simply more mixed. In contrast, evidence suggests that Asian American students experience the lowest rates of suspension when controlling for gender (Wallace et al., 2008).

LACK OF EVIDENCE ON BEHAVIORAL DIFFERENCES AMONG STUDENTS

One clear finding from the research on disproportionate disciplinary actions taken against Black students: the offenses for which Black students are suspended are not any more dangerous or violent than the offenses for which White students are charged, who are much less likely to receive out-of-school suspension. After reviewing over 183 studies published between 1990 and 2017, Welsh and Little concluded that "race is one of the most significant predictors of OSS [out-of-school suspension] regardless of behavior." They also found that even after accounting for class differences among students, race is "a significant predictor" of receiving exclusionary discipline (Welsh & Little, 2018, p. 757). In other words, Black students are neither more likely to engage in dangerous nor in violent conduct, but they are more likely to receive an out-of-school suspension for their violation.

This issue of how prevalent dangerous or violent conduct is among students is an important one, particularly since it taps into prevalent myths and stereotypes about Black criminality. There are two ways of examining whether Black or White students are engaging in more dangerous or risky behavior. First, you can rely on surveys of students, asking them if and how often they engage in violent, threatening, or risky behaviors (e.g., bringing a knife to school, getting into fights, or bullying other students). Second, you can rely on misconduct reports filed by teachers and/or principals laying out the disruptive behavior. Scholars who have studied the issue from either the student or the administrative perspective have found little difference between Black and White propensity for dangerous or violent behaviors. As one group of scholars wrote, "Studies using both measures of student self-report and extant school disciplinary records . . . have generally failed to find evidence of racial differences in student behavior. In short, there appears to be a notable paucity of evidence that could support a hypothesis that the racial discipline gap can be explained through differential rates of misbehavior" (Gregory et al., 2010, p. 62). Welsh and Little concluded, similarly, that "the evidence indicates that the higher rates of exclusionary discipline experienced by Black students are not the result of higher rates of misbehavior or these students engaging in a greater variety of infractions or more severe infractions" (Welsh & Little, 2018, p. 760).

CLASSROOM EXCHANGES AND THE RESORT TO DISCIPLINE

Let's dig a little deeper into the kinds of conduct for which Black students receive suspension. According to Russell Skiba, a social psychologist and a leading researcher on exclusionary school discipline, "Racial disparities in school discipline begin with classroom referral and classroom management" (Skiba, 2015, p. 111). That is, the teacher's initial decision to refer a student to the principal's office starts the ball rolling, and if that decision is racially inflected, over time, hundreds of those decisions add up to a racially skewed disciplinary process.

> The teacher's initial decision to refer a student to the principal's office starts the ball rolling, and if that decision is racially inflected, over time, hundreds of those decisions add up to a racially skewed disciplinary process.

Research into the discretionary act of teachers to send a student down the hall has shown some compelling patterns. Vavrus and Cole (2002) examined videotapes of a full semester of two high school science classes, along with researchers' in-person classroom observations in a Midwestern city that had seen dramatic White flight over the twenty years prior. The demographic breakdown of the student body was 60 percent Latinx, 20 percent African American, 10 percent White, 8 percent Asian, and 2 percent Native American. Jefferson High School also had a significant number of students in poverty, with 75 percent of its students qualifying for free or reduced-price lunch.

By examining videotapes, Vavrus and Cole (2002) traced out the series of interactions between students and teachers that led, ultimately, to the student being referred to Jefferson High School's administration for disciplinary action. In the wake of a death of a student in the school hallways the prior spring, a new principal took an activist stance and visible presence in the school hallways, instituting a strict new hall passing policy. Any student without a school ID and a hall pass during class hours was escorted to the school detention area and immediately issued a suspension. Many teachers supported the new activist stance and the adoption of a new suspension policy, ostensibly aimed at curbing the intrusion of community violence into the school. The new policy also mandated a zero tolerance "for a serious breach of discipline." All infractions would result in a suspension. While the staff handbook did not provide any examples of what constituted a "serious breach of discipline," students were required to sign a form indicating that they were aware of the new disciplinary policy, which stated that students would be suspended for any of the following: gang activity; fighting; use or possession of weapons, alcohol, or drugs; verbal abuse; repeated classroom disruption; chronic violation of any combination of school rules.

In operation, the new policy became a tool of classroom management at Jefferson High School, according to Vavrus and Cole (2002). In one example, a first-year teacher who had the highest number of suspensions within the school responded to persistent student questions by ignoring them, thinking this was an effective strategy to get the class to listen attentively. One day, as tensions mounted because of the teacher's refusal to respond directly to students' questions until all the students were silent, a student uttered a side comment disputing the need to understand math in a science class. The teacher responded by summoning security aides to remove that student from the classroom. As Vavrus and Cole write, it was not any moment of violence or a provocative act that prompted the removal; rather it was "the teacher's interpretation of a particular utterance as hostile or disruptive that precipitated the removal of a student from the classroom" (2002).

Much hinged here on the teacher's inability to manage a classroom and perceiving student confusion about why math is important to science as a direct challenge to his pedagogical authority. The suspension did not serve any need to prevent violence or because the student possessed any drugs or weapons. Rather the suspension compensated for a teacher's inability to engage students and to effectively manage the classroom. In focus groups, the researchers interviewed the students about their impressions of the classroom, including some who had been suspended. A suspended student explained, "They [teachers] get frustrated at the class and whoever is the last person to talk, oh there you go, bye bye. . . . You know you not going to say the last word. You're going to get sent out" (Vavrus & Cole, 2002, p. 1040). In the conclusion to their study, Vavrus and Cole state what should be clear by now:

"It is in moment-by-moment interactions that decisions are made about who may stay in class and who will be suspended."

The importance of race to those moment-by-moment interactions cannot be overstated. The cultural cues, the rhetorical expectations, the differing assumptions students and teachers make about when it is appropriate to interrupt, to insist on silence, to challenge authority—all of these are racially imbued. These encounters present teachers with a responsibility to understand the cross-cultural and cross-racial differences between themselves and their students. Compounding that difficulty is the large and growing racial imbalance between the racial identity of the US teaching force and the racial identities of students in US schools. Roughly 75 percent of US public school teachers are White females (Ingersoll, 2019), while BIPOC students currently comprise 53 percent of the pre-K–12 enrollment (US Department of Education, 2021). Unless school leaders and teachers develop an antiracist perspective, as well as cultural competence and cross-racial communication skills, school discipline will remain racially imbalanced and skewed for at least a generation. The fact that most teacher preparation programs lack systemic training in cultural competence and inter-racial dialogue is a significant component of the school-to-prison pipeline and needs significant and urgent attention.

Teacher programs across the country are not preparing future teachers for working with children from diverse backgrounds. Furthermore, colleges and schools of education need to ensure that future teachers receive the appropriate training to understand their biases and counteract the stereotypes they have internalized about BIPOC children. This lack of training perpetuates the systemic racism that is pervasive in schools across the United States. Many novice teachers enter classrooms that serve BIPOC students and they've never had an experience with BIPOC students prior to their teaching assignment. Without a coherent program through which teacher candidates gain this experience and expertise, the statistics concerning racial disparities in school discipline are unlikely to change. Better teacher training is the first step in dismantling the school-to-prison pipeline.

THE ROLE OF ZERO TOLERANCE POLICIES

A teacher's decision to make a referral to the school administration's office for disciplinary action is only a part, however, of the school discipline policy context. What happens to that student, and the discretion that an administrator has to evaluate context and motive, are constrained by federal, state, and local regulations. Since the late 1980s and early 1990s, "zero tolerance" policies have dominated this policy environment. Defined as policies that are "intended primarily as a method of sending a message that certain behaviors will not be tolerated, by punishing all offenses severely, no matter how minor" (Skiba & Knesting, p. 20), zero tolerance in school discipline arose as concerns about youth violence and school shootings dominated the media. Although juvenile crime peaked in 1994 and began a long downward trend thereafter (Kang-Brown et al., 2013, p. 2), in the mid-1990s, newspaper headlines were full of references to "super-predators" and sensationalistic stories of youth, particularly Black youth, run amok. In 1996, then–Princeton University professor John DiIulio wrote an article in the conservative magazine *The Weekly Standard*, issuing dire predictions about the coming wave of youth violence and callous indifference. In one passage, DiIulio related an interview with a Philadelphia district attorney. In breathless tones, DiIulio wrote:

> We're not just talking about teenagers. . . . We're talking about boys whose voices have yet to change. We're talking about elementary school youngsters who pack guns instead of lunches. We're talking about kids who have absolutely no respect for human life and no sense of the future. In short, we're talking big trouble that hasn't yet begun to crest (DiIulio, 1995).

The media fervor justified the extension of zero tolerance policies to a wide range of activities—all of which now required mandatory suspension. In 1994, President Clinton signed into law the Gun-Free School Zones Act, which required all school districts receiving federal funds to impose a mandatory one-year suspension on any student who carried a firearm onto school grounds, plus a mandatory referral to the criminal or juvenile justice system. From there, the mandatory punishments spread to other misconduct: by 1997, 94 percent of all schools had zero tolerance, mandatory penalties for firearms, 87 percent for alcohol, and 79 percent for violence or tobacco (Skiba & Knesting, 2002, p. 20).

The adoption of zero tolerance policies not only subjected vastly greater numbers of students to suspension, it also forced principals and superintendents to defend irrational and wholly unjust applications of disciplinary policies. In Atlanta, Georgia, an eleven-year-old was suspended for two weeks because her Tweety Bird wallet had a ten-inch toy chain that connected to her key ring. Because the weapons policy defined all chains as weapons, just like pellet guns, ice picks, and swords, she was barred from school (Skiba and Knesting, 2002, p. 22). In Alexandria, Louisiana, a second grader brought his grandfather's pocket watch to school for show and tell. Because it had a one-inch pocket knife attached, he was suspended and sent to an alternative school for one month. In San Diego, a twelve-year-old was expelled from school because he violated the ban on fighting. It turns out that he scuffled with classmates after they called him "fat." A six-year-old in Colorado Springs who shared some organic lemon drops with friends on the playground was suspended for possessing "other chemical substances." A nine-year old in Virginia was suspended for handing out Certs Concentrated Mints in class; he was interviewed by a police officer and was found to have possessed and distributed "look alike drugs" (Skiba and Peterson, 1999, Table 2, p. 375). The adoption of zero tolerance policies—and their extension beyond possession or use of firearms—produced patently absurd school actions and showed the dangers of rigid and inflexible disciplinary policies. Zero tolerance policies prevent decision-makers from engaging the contexts of the infraction, the severity of the harm, the motive, or even the cognitive and developmental ability of students to understand why they are being punished. The emotional and psychological effects of zero tolerance policies, particularly for vulnerable students, can be immense. In Fairfax, Virginia, a student-athlete committed suicide after being suspended for buying synthetic marijuana, a legal but "imitation controlled substance." His death, along with the suicide of another Fairfax County student-athlete suspended a year earlier, prompted calls for reforming Fairfax's disciplinary policies, which some called "too lengthy, too rigid, and too hostile" (St. George, 2011).

Zero tolerance policies are now under close examination and many school systems are scaling back the extent of these policies, but they remain in effect in many school systems and states throughout the nation. Part of the argument against maintaining these rigid and inflexible rules—beyond their disparate racial impacts—is that they simply don't work. Russell Skiba, a leading scholar on school disciplinary policies, concluded that zero tolerance policies create worse, not better, learning environments for students: "No data exist to show that out-of-school suspensions and expulsions reduce disruption or improve school climate. If anything, disciplinary removal appears to have negative effects on student outcomes and the learning climate" (Skiba, 2014). The American Psychological Association's Zero Tolerance Task Force concluded in 2008 that

Zero tolerance has not been shown to improve school climate or school safety. Its application in suspension and expulsion has not proven an effective means of improving student behavior. It has not resolved, and may have exacerbated, minority over-representation in school punishments (American Psychological Association, 2008, p. 113).

The school shootings at Columbine High School, Sandy Hook Elementary School, and Marjory Stoneman Douglas High School—and countless others—have prompted district officials, politicians, and school leaders to adopt and expand zero tolerance policies when those policies would have done (and did) little to stop these horrific and senseless deaths. (Indeed, the shooter at Marjory Stoneman Douglas High School had been expelled from the school.) Zero tolerance are performative policies that do not address the underlying cause of dangerous or harmful behaviors, shunt the problems onto other institutions, and profoundly harm students and their families. To be an antiracist school leader is to challenge at every opportunity the use of zero tolerance policies within schools. They remove professional skill and discretion from schools, sever the opportunities schools have to maintain constructive ties with students who are teetering on the edge of dropping out, and make students mistrust the adults in their lives.

THE CONSEQUENCES OF SUSPENSION: LESS LIKELY TO GRADUATE

For the almost three million students suspended every year, the time away from school is not simply time to catch up on TV watching. Suspended students have much worse educational outcomes than non-suspended students. Researchers have debated whether suspended students suffer worse outcomes because they were already in a precarious educational position (low grades, spotty attendance, lack of engagement) *prior* to the suspension or whether the suspensions themselves contributed to those worse educational outcomes. The answer is becoming increasingly clear: suspensions have a significant negative and independent effect on student learning and attainment.

In a rigorous study of New York City suspension policies, Chu and Ready (2018) compared student performance during semesters that students received a suspension against those

Students who received at least one suspension in the first three semesters of high school were 10–12% less likely to pass a New York State Regents exam, 17% less likely to graduate from high school in four years, and 16% less likely to graduate within 5 or 6 years.

semesters in which the same student did not receive a suspension. They found that students who received a principal's suspension (fewer than five days) passed 3 percent fewer math and 4 percent fewer English credits and were 2 percent more likely to drop out the following semester (Chu and Ready, 2018, p. 494). While these short-term effects may not seem like much, they accumulate over time. In fact, the longer-term impacts of suspension (particularly in the early years of high school) were more damaging to students: students who received at least one suspension in the first three semesters of high school were 10–12 percent less likely to pass a New York State Regents exam, 17 percent less likely to graduate from high school in four years, and 16 percent less likely to graduate within five or six years (compared to students who were estimated to be equally likely to have received a suspension, but did not, based on background and behavioral characteristics). A 17 percent reduction in likelihood of graduation was by far the largest effect size among all the factors explored in the study. In other words, among all the factors used to predict a student's likelihood of graduating, having at least one suspension in the first three years of high school had the biggest influence (Chu and Ready, 2018).

Other studies have consistently found negative educational outcomes to be associated with suspension: higher dropout rates, lower grades, lower test scores, less academic engagement, and additional suspensions later in school (Suh et al., 2014; Lee et al., 2011; Hwang, 2018; Morris & Perry, 2016). Suspended students obviously spend less time engaging with academic material and are more likely to develop negative or hostile views toward school, reducing the relational bonds that are crucial both to academic and personal development. No study has found that suspension improves the academic outcomes of suspended students. One longitudinal study found that students who were suspended for the first time in the 1995–96 school year were 24 percent less likely to have earned a BA twelve years after the suspension than similar non-suspended students (Rosenbaum, 2020). Another study estimated that roughly 20 percent of the achievement gap between White and Black students is due to the academic effects of suspension and the racial disproportionality in the use of out-of-school suspension (Morris & Perry, 2016).

Restorative Practice

Oakland, California

Born in Birmingham, Alabama, Fania Davis was a teenager when a pipe bomb tore through the 16th St. Baptist Church on Sunday September 15, 1963, killing four young girls: fourteen-year-olds Addie Mae Collins, Denise McNair, and Carole Robertson and eleven-year-old Cynthia Wesley. Two of those girls were close friends of Fania Davis. Coming of age during the civil rights movement and the violent backlash against it, Ms. Davis (later Dr. Davis) was inspired by the movements for change all around her. She became a leader in the civil rights movement, the Black liberation movement, the women's movement, and the anti-apartheid movement. Earning her law degree from UC Berkeley she practiced civil rights law for 27 years.

In 2005, nearing sixty, at an age when many people are looking toward retirement, Fania Davis cofounded Restorative Justice for Oakland Youth (RJOY) and became its director in 2008. RJOY's mission is to change how communities and schools respond when youth engage in harmful behavior—harmful to others or to themselves. Committed to shifting the narrative from punitive responses to restorative practices, RJOY worked with a transformative school leader who was disillusioned with existing school disciplinary practices and established a pilot project at a single middle school in West Oakland, Cole Middle School.

Within two years, Cole saw an 87 percent reduction in school suspension rates and improved academic outcomes. In 2010, Oakland Unified School District adopted restorative justice as its official school disciplinary policy. Within eight years, roughly forty schools in the district employed restorative practice.

RJOY's model of restorative justice uses a three-tiered approach. Tier One engages the entire school community in training, coaching, and facilitation of both one-on-one "restorative conversations" and "community building circles" (Davis, 2018). The goal in Tier One is to build shared values and skills to create a culture of healing and relationship-building to shift the school climate. Restorative circles allow participants (students, teachers, and staff) to build shared values about how to engage in conversations; these values are used as collective discussion techniques even outside of a disciplinary context. Shared values such as listening, respect for one another, not

(Continued)

(Continued)

interrupting, and participating fully become both expectations and resources for the community (Sumner et al., 2010).

Tier Two involves training, coaching, and facilitation to address conflict after it emerges. These Tier Two interventions serve as alternatives to out-of-school suspensions, but they can also be used for other disciplinary issues. Tier Three addresses the needs of individual students and the community to welcome and reintegrate a student back to school after an absence, perhaps caused by incarceration or other reason for a student's separation from school.

In RJOY's formulation, "the essence of restorative justice involves shifting the locus of power from systems and professionals to communities and ordinary people" (Davis, 2018). In practice, this means giving students and teachers the respect and autonomy to both express the sense of harm and injury to the wrongdoer but also to undertake a healing in conjunction with the wrong-doer to repair the relationship.

SUSPENSION LEADS INTO THE JUVENILE JUSTICE SYSTEM

Not only are the academic futures of students imperiled when they are suspended, their very freedom is at risk. The disciplinary system within schools is increasingly connected to the juvenile justice system, both formally and informally. The growing presence of police officers on school grounds—which jumped substantially in the wake of highly visible school shootings such as Columbine High School in 1999—transforms every act of student misbehavior into a possible arrest. Moreover, schools have increasingly been required to refer school disciplinary matters to police for investigation and possible arrest. Finally, the sheer number of students pushed out of school through out-of-school suspensions and expulsions produces a greater pool of youth with no constructive activity to engage them—a recipe for bad outcomes that frequently involve the police. One study found that adolescents who were suspended were over twice as likely to be arrested in the month of suspension, compared to the months when the adolescent was not suspended or expelled from school (Monahan et al., 2014). Another longitudinal study found that if a Black youth were suspended, they were 58 percent more likely to have been arrested at least once within 12 years after the suspension, compared to similar Black youth who had not been suspended. Among all youth, 12 years after suspension, suspended students were 23 percent more likely to have been to prison than non-suspended youth (Rosenbaum, 2020). All told, the growing numbers of police on school grounds, mandatory referrals to police, and the burgeoning numbers of suspended and expelled students laid the foundations for the rapid expansion of the school to prison pipeline in the 1990s and early 2000s.

> The growing numbers of police on school grounds, mandatory referrals to police, and the burgeoning numbers of suspended and expelled students laid the foundations for the rapid expansion of the school to prison pipeline in the 1990s and early 2000s.

The racial disparities in school disciplinary systems are amplified within the criminal justice system. Homer and Fisher (2020), examining a national database of student arrests, found that having police on school grounds is associated with more student arrests than no police on school grounds and having police on school grounds yields more arrests of Black boys than any other student demographic. More police equals more arrests and, just as with suspensions, Black boys bear the brunt of the policy.

RECONCEIVING SCHOOL DISCIPLINE

There are a number of steps school leaders, parents, and teachers can take to change the culture of discipline within schools. What is needed is a move away from the command-and-control model of the criminal justice system and the construction of disciplinary processes and priorities within schools that promote the well-being and learning of all students including those charged with misconduct. A commitment to learning, including behavioral learning, should be the hallmark of an effective and fair disciplinary structure.

STEP 1: LIMIT OUT-OF-SCHOOL SUSPENSIONS

While the numbers of out-of-school suspensions have gone down over the past decade, there is no evidence that the racial imbalances in out-of-school suspensions have shifted. So, while the recent reductions in the total number of suspensions is a good first step, the existing disparities need to be reversed as well. School leaders need to devise alternatives to out-of-school suspensions in order to limit the racial consequences of a skewed disciplinary technique.

STEP 2: ANALYZE THE RACIAL DISPARITIES IN DISCIPLINARY DECISIONS AND ENGAGE IN CULTURALLY SUSTAINING AND RESTORATIVE PRACTICES TO BUILD RELATIONSHIPS BETWEEN STUDENTS AND STAFF

Your commitment to make your disciplinary system antiracist means looking explicitly at the racial drivers of disparities in disciplinary actions and, at the same time, engaging in culturally sustaining and restorative practices to establish the needed relationships and bond with students required to build trust and mutual respect. If racial bias—implicit or otherwise—seems to be a part of the disciplinary dynamic, from tensions among students to teacher referrals to administrative discretion and decision-making, it is essential that you engage with that issue directly. We provide some advice in Chapter 3, Stage 2: Discovery about the kinds of questions school leaders and staff need to ask in order to broach these difficult conversations and to keep them on a constructive plane. It is hard and necessary work, and it works best when you focus on the systemic issues that are preventing students from experiencing educational equity and realizing their full potential. Through culturally sustaining and responsive approaches to student well-being, you will help foster a climate of mutual respect within schools—respect for students, for their families, their communities, and their cultural anchors. That respect will allow more positive, supportive, and antiracist policies to emerge.

STEP 3: ENGAGE ALL STAKEHOLDERS, INCLUDING STUDENTS, IN CONSTRUCTING ANTIRACIST DISCIPLINARY PRACTICES

Engage the problem holistically, not just as a problem of student behavior. Engage multiple stakeholders in this process of constructing an antiracist set of disciplinary practices: students, families, guardians, teachers, school administrators, community leaders, coaches, central office personnel, staff, security personnel, school nurses, facilities maintenance personnel, religious leaders and pastors, and any other adults within or outside schools who can forge bonds with students. These multiple views on the lives of students can shed light on underlying issues that may not be evident to teachers and principals.

ACTION STEPS FOR DEVELOPING AN ANTIRACIST DISCIPLINARY SYSTEM

☐ Establish data systems that enable school officials to look at patterns among disciplinary referrals by teachers, including teacher experience, teacher and student racial identity, nature of misconduct, and frequency of disciplinary referrals, student, and teacher accounts of misconduct.

☐ Examine your disciplinary cases for patterns of referrals (time of year, nature of misconduct, class period, referring teachers) and strive to identify and reduce the largest clusters of referrals through focused interventions on classroom management.

☐ Include within your professional development program, the aggregate data for your school or system on the role of race in the disciplinary process and the historical and continuing discrepancies in the application of discipline. Making teachers aware of that aggregate level of performance can prompt necessary self-reflection on their own role within the disciplinary process.

☐ Cultivate in teachers, particularly among White teachers, both racial self-awareness and culturally responsive teaching strategies that foster productive relationships between students and teachers.

☐ At the middle and high school levels, ask for student input and participation in the construction of a student discipline policy. This could include peer juries or classroom and community circles to address harms or conflicts among students.

☐ Consider the adoption of an array of restorative practices that focus repairing the relations that are harmed when a student engages in misconduct. Through small group conversations, peer adjudications, student-written honor and conduct codes, disciplinary systems can move away from a punitive frame and toward the promotion of desired behaviors and habits.

☐ Consider the implementation of school-wide positive behavior interventions and supports (PBIS). These practices seek to promote and encourage positive student actions, rather than punish undesired behaviors. A holistic engagement of all the factors that influence student behaviors, PBIS-based approaches have been shown empirically to reduce the use of suspensions, although they have not, on their own, reduced the racial gap in disciplinary actions taken against students.

CONCLUSION

The school to prison pipeline was built on racially skewed suspensions and the growing presence of police officers actively patrolling school grounds. To construct an antiracist disciplinary system means (1) devising a strategy to eliminate the disparities between the punishments that BIPOC students receive and the punishment that White students receive and (2) devising an alternative to police enforcement on school grounds. Those who defend the use of suspensions and school resource officers have, at best, a narrow and limited evidence base that these practices improve learning environments for students. The bulk of research shows that they are self-defeating policies that undo the good work of teachers, parents, students, staff, and administrators as they educate the next generation. Antiracist work in schools requires creating better systems to ensure the safety, well-being, and learning of all students. The place to start is to move away from a focus on punishment and to foster positive student actions and to restore relationships when they are strained by conflict or misconduct. John Lewis himself could not find a better place to get into Good Trouble than in the detention hall.

5

Tips for Adopting Restorative Practice

A University of California, Berkeley Law School report on Cole Middle School found significant changes in school climate and declines in the use of suspension after the adoption of restorative practice. At the same time, it offered guidance for schools considering adopting RJOY's practices (Sumner et al., 2010):

- Be prepared to invest time and energy, particularly during the initial phases.

- Be clear on the purpose of restorative activities and avoid overuse.

- Gain support from those at the school.

- Focus on the principles that inform the actual practices of restorative justice.

- Clarify when activities are fully restorative, partially restorative, or not part of the restorative justice program.

- Be prepared for changes in school culture due to the increased student responsibility and voice.
- Involve adults who understand adolescents and who respect community norms, values, and cultures present at the school.
- Understand that relationship continuity is important to sustaining a school-based restorative justice program.
- Involve adults who have a nuanced understanding of the larger community and acceptance by that community.
- Recognize and address the negative assumptions some people make about the characteristics of others.

By shifting the frame of school discipline from one that imposes punishment as a corrective for transgressive behavior to one that seeks to address the underlying roots of that behavior, restorative practice can be one way to make school discipline less like policing.

Reflective Questions for Making School Discipline Different From Policing

1. **Personal Reflections**

   - How would you summarize your personal philosophy about student discipline and the ways in which current policies and practices need modification or transformation in your school or school system?
   - Does your disciplinary system help strengthen personal trust and connection between students and staff? Does it make students feel safe and secure in school?

2. **Organizational Insights**

   - As you reflect upon your current learning organization, what do student disciplinary data reveal about potential or existing inequities requiring immediate attention?

3. **Initial Steps**

   - What kinds of conversations and professional learning activities might be useful in beginning the process of making

(Continued)

(Continued)

school discipline different from "policing"? In your experience, are staff members with whom you work aware of the implications of inequitable disciplinary practices and trends and their impact upon minority students?

4. **Long-Range Possibilities**

   - What would a day in the life of a student look like in a learning environment that promotes positive student–teacher exchanges and equitable disciplinary practices?

   - What are the key multiyear action steps that will be necessary to achieve the vision you are articulating?

5. **Anticipated Barriers and Challenges**

   - How will you enlist students and parents in this process of developing an equitable disciplinary system? Why are their insights, recommendations, and voices such a critical part of this process?

CHAPTER 6

Implement Strategic Thinking and Strategic Planning

GUIDING PRINCIPLES

1. Antiracist school leaders develop an effective strategic plan as a road map for transformation.

2. Antiracist school leaders design strategic plans that support their equity agenda. Their plans are informed by a collective mission and vision for racial equity in which every student succeeds.

3. Antiracist school leaders work off of strategic plans that are continuously updated road maps aimed at realizing their vision for equity.

4. Antiracist school leaders create well-articulated, equity-driven strategic plans that include key performance indicators, necessary resources, clearly articulated timeline, explicit roles and responsibilities, and a sustainable communication plan.

THE BEST LAID PLANS . . .

Any plan a school leader had in place at the beginning of March 2020 was torn to shreds three weeks later. Ideas about lengthening recess or building new community–school partnerships were hopelessly irrelevant in the face of the COVID-19-induced shutdown of US schools. The pandemic, and the accompanying death and illness, has revealed the extent to which structural inequities continue to plague our educational system. From a lack of universal student access to high-speed internet and other technology resources to the tragic ways in which socio-economically disadvantaged families have confronted food insecurity and housing crises during the pandemic, the events of 2020 and 2021 validated that schools must continue to act as resources for the communities they serve. It is incumbent on school leaders to bring staff together to help resolve issues of disproportionality, inequity, and systemic racism that affect the families and students within our communities. To undertake those tasks, school leaders need to build their professional capacity to engage in strategic planning and strategic thinking. Together with resources, strategic planning and thinking are remarkable tools to bring together educators, students, families, and communities to address our needs.

This chapter urges you to take strategic planning and strategic thinking seriously and to undertake these efforts with courage and boldness. As part of our urging, we want to stress that strategic plans should not just sit on a shelf, waiting for the next pandemic or calamity to arise. The strategic plans of school systems need to be organic, living documents that guide and inform the application of principles and strategies to enhance the daily educational life of students and staff. Equity and anti-racism must be essential focus areas for any effective strategic plan. At the same time, such plans must be designed to engage all stakeholders in the crucial conversations that are the life-blood of equity transformation in school systems. A strategic plan must be an ever-evolving document that is understood, refined, articulated, supported, and reaffirmed by all members of a learning organization.

WAYS TO THINK ABOUT STRATEGIC PLANS

Would you go on a road trip without your road map, the global positioning system (GPS), or cell phone? Would you head to the airport to catch a flight without having your airline, departure time, boarding pass, and identification at the ready? Would you throw a party for someone without inviting guests or ensuring that the guests had your address? It may feel more carefree to head out on a road trip without prior planning, but when you're undertaking a complex initiative within an organization, funded by other people's money, it's in your best interests to develop a plan. On your journey to becoming an antiracist school leader, strategic thinking and a robust strategic plan will guide you through uncharted waters.

To eliminate achievement and opportunity gaps for marginalized students, it is imperative to look beyond the mission and vision of the organization and focus on strategy to attain your goals. *Strategic thinking* is to anticipate the reaction of others to actions you undertake. *Strategic planning* is to have a plan of action to respond to those anticipated reactions of others. Your plan cannot be thrown together haphazardly; a methodical and strategic approach is key.

An effective *strategic plan* for racial equity is both a road map for transformation as well as your best understanding of the challenges and changing contexts you will confront as you implement that transformation. The plan's design should be guided and informed by a collective mission and vision for racial equity, drawing on the reflective process we outlined in Chapter 3, and its primary objective should be that every student succeeds no matter what their life's circumstances. Too many strategic plans are simply an exercise in paper, something that is completed for purposes of compliance and conformity to local and state requirements. To avoid that fate, your strategic plan needs the following components: mission, vision, core values, theory of practice, strategic goals with action steps, key performance indicators, and a robust communications and reporting strategy. A good strategic plan needs to *do* a number of things, as well. Let's quickly review the parts first and then we'll examine a good strategic plan's tasks.

START WITH MISSION AND VISION . . . BUT DON'T STOP THERE

At the foundation of an effective strategic plan lies a well-articulated mission and vision statement for your school system with clearly expressed core values for the individual learner as well as the means by which the school system will address the needs of the whole child (including their social, emotional, and academic learning needs). The process of defining, refining, and adopting a mission and vision statement—along with the core values that support them—will increase community buy-in and boost your opportunity for success, particularly when done through an inclusive and representative process.

You will need to develop a set of guiding principles that inform the realization of your mission and vision. The challenge here is to articulate how that vision and mission will come into being. These may include the adoption of culturally responsive pedagogies or you might rely on accountability-driven strategies and practices that emphasize personalization, differentiation, and supports to maximize the achievement of all learners. The components of your school system's theory of practice should be informed by what the best research indicates is most suited to your students and your community. A theory of practice that does not comport with the circumstances of your school system is not a terribly good theory, making it harder to realize the substantive goals you've adopted. So, know your school system, its students, its community, and the people on your team and devise a theory of practice (or theories of practice, if needed) that is appropriate for your contexts.

After you and your team have arrived at a clear understanding of your methodology and your theory of practice, you will need to clarify what, exactly, your goals are. Generally, these goals are defined as SMART (specific, measurable, actionable, relevant, and timely) goals, but since you have been developing this strategic plan with data systems in mind and in response to clear needs within your community and school system, the goals you will most likely hit upon will already be SMART enough. But make sure that you can articulate them in keeping with the SMART convention, if only to make them clear and transparent and worthwhile to all your stakeholders.

Next, your system will need to arrive at some agreement on navigation. You will need to decide not just who is flying the plane, but what instruments will you rely upon to help you understand where you are. As the components of your plan begin to form, identify the indicators and metrics you and your team will utilize to determine if you are remaining on course. You need to decide what aspects of the system's performance needs to be on the dashboard in order for you to see the effects of the transformation you are undertaking. These key performance indicators also utilize underlying measurement tools to capture and report the data you want. Sometimes this data comes from ongoing assessments (either formative or summative) and sometimes they might emerge from student or staffing surveys. The right metrics and the right measurement tools will vary across school systems. The work you've done in articulating your school system's equity and antiracist goals should form key elements of this navigational system.

You will need to decide what instruments will you rely upon to help you understand where you are Identify the indicators and metrics you and your team will utilize to determine if you are remaining on course.

Once you have a clear understanding of what metrics and key performance indicators you will use (and the data tools that deliver the information to you), you will need to arrive at the targets your plan will be aiming at for each of those key performance indicators. That process may be difficult, and it will certainly require a close collaboration with staff and school-based personnel. Without reasonable targets, staff might feel demoralized; without ambitious targets, there won't

ELEMENTS OF A STRATEGIC PLAN

☐ **Mission and vision statements**: These collaboratively drafted statements identify the aspirational and integral components of a school system. They assert the distinctive features of the school system and its people within it that best represent what it stands for, as well as the kind of organization the community would like it to become.

☐ **Core values**: Also collaboratively expressed, these principles organize and sustain the daily work of the school system, its community members, leadership, and staff.

☐ **Theory of practice**: This articulation defines the means and methodology by which the school system will realize its core values, mission, and vision in the work that it undertakes. The theory of practice commits the school system to a particular approach as it seeks to achieve its goals for its students, staff, and families, typically anchored in a body of research supported by empirical evidence of effectiveness.

☐ **Strategic goal with action steps**: These goals specifically identify the concrete actions to be undertaken, in keeping with the theory of practice, that you and your team feel has the greatest likelihood of realizing your vision and mission, while remaining true to your core values. Often these goals are identified as SMART (specific, measurable, actionable, relevant, and timely) goals, but the strategic planning process typically ensures that goals produced within the plan already have those characteristics.

☐ **Key performance indicators**: These metrics, collected uniformly via well-developed measurement tools, guide decision-makers and are used to ascertain progress toward clearly expressed targets and are also used make midcourse adjustments by school and school system personnel.

☐ **Targets**: These benchmarks indicate whether progress is being made on the key performance indicators.

☐ **Inventory of Resources**: These are the assets, materials, and labor required to undertake the agreed upon theory of practice in order to meet the performance targets.

☐ **Assigned responsibilities and timeline**: This is a clear and detailed delineation of which individuals or teams are responsible for which set of activities or milestones, at any given time.

(Continued)

(Continued)

> ☐ **Monitoring and reporting system**: The method used to report the results of activities and milestones, along with key performance indicators, to all relevant stakeholders and personnel to ascertain whether progress is being made on the system goals.

be a strong sense of urgency. Let your understanding of what bold and courageous leadership means be your guide here.

Three other elements form the basis of any self-respecting strategic plan. First, you will need to articulate the necessary resources to hit your performance targets. If those resources are unavailable or not forthcoming, you may need to revisit your performance targets. You'll need to assign roles and responsibilities to specific individuals or teams, along with a sharply delineated timeline of activities and milestones for them to accomplish. Finally, you will need to work across your team to develop a system of monitoring and reporting the results of those activities—along with the key progress indicators—and to disseminate those reports to all personnel who need them to undertake their own work.

WHAT A STRATEGIC PLAN MUST DO

Beyond assembling all the components of a strategic plan, many of which can be quite complex, you must also pay attention to what the plan is *doing*. That a plan is not simply a product but an active agent, undertaking work, is an important point we want to emphasize. The reason we want you to think of the plan as an actor, working alongside you, is that this principle forms the basis of strategic thinking.

Let's explain this by thinking about the metaphors commonly used to describe a strategic plan: a road map, an itinerary, a list of activities. All of these metaphors capture some element of a strategic plan—they all convey a sense that a strategic plan helps us get somewhere or do something new. Those metaphors are all anchored in the understanding that executing the plan does not change the context of the plan. In other words, if we follow the road map, the roads don't move. Or if we keep to our itinerary, the sights we are seeing along the way don't change. *But if a strategic plan is truly effective, it will change the world, or at least the contexts in which the plan is operating.* Think about it: if our strategic plan is aimed at reducing the number of students who wind up in the juvenile justice system, there will be less need for correctional officers within the juvenile justice system. If our strategic plan shrinks that population, there will be consequences. That's what the plan is doing and that's what you need to keep track of and plan for.

This is where strategic thinking comes into play. Strategic thinking is understanding how others will react in response to our moves. What will my chess-playing opponent do if I capture their rook? How will I be made vulnerable or how will my position be strengthened? That is the crux of strategic thinking, and strategic plans lay the foundation for a vast terrain of strategic thinking, if the plan is successful.

LINKING STRATEGIC THINKING TO STRATEGIC PLANNING

The first and the most simple step of undertaking strategic thinking alongside the strategic planning process is to pay attention to the cycle of strategic planning. Most stories have a beginning, middle, and an end, but with strategic planning there is only, really, a beginning, a middle, a review, and a new beginning. That cycle also attaches to the regular calendar of a school system and the budget cycle of either the school system or the county or city it lies within. Remember the step in the strategic planning process we described above that talked about identifying resources you will need to achieve your goals? That process of generating resources needs to be in sync with your city or county's process of budget allocation. You need to understand how the officials who have control over the purse strings will react to your requests for new money, if you are in a school system that is fiscally dependent.

Other elements of the calendar are equally pertinent to strategic thinking and strategic planning. Often a strategic plan also drives the annual school system's areas of focus, including the superintendent's goals and expectations in their annual evaluation. In addition, the strategic plan's performance targets are also often tied to staff evaluations, ensuring shared accountability and commitment to the plan's principles and performance targets. Therefore, this commitment to accountability should guide the school improvement planning process, providing schools with the outcomes they should be seeking as a learning community. At the same time, it is essential that the voices and perspectives of all stakeholder groups (from students to staff to the board and community members) be included in the design and implementation of both the system-level strategic plan and every school improvement plan. Thus, the timing and emphasis of a strategic plan requires strategic thinking in advance.

PAY ATTENTION TO ALIGNMENT

Another realm in which strategic thinking bolsters strategic planning is alignment, or the process by which school-based personnel and central office personnel are able to work in common toward a jointly defined goal. In effect, these two groups must share a common vision and work collaboratively to address the key performance indicators for which they are accountable. Too often, educators at the school level see administrators working too far from student concerns to have clear sense of the daily challenges confronting teachers and students. Teachers in the classroom may be focused, because of accountability pressures, on academic outcomes and feel that central office endeavors to focus on antiracism initiatives or systemic injustices are not connected to efforts to improve instruction. As the preceding chapters have shown, however, there is a startling range of problems of practice that schools and school systems must confront if racial equity is to be fully realized, including disproportionality data involving student academic underachievement, BIPOC lack of access and engagement in higher-level programs, wildly disproportionate suspension and expulsion rates, and overall lack of educational opportunity related to the preparation of students for postsecondary education and the world of work. Central office strategic plans that are too removed from the daily routines of teachers will inevitably fail because the lack of alignment will lead to teachers lying low until the latest reform fad fades. Strategic thinking means that you understand what the reactions of teachers will be as you implement the strategic plan *and* that you have a clear idea of what your response will be when they respond to the plan. A strategic understanding of alignment will go a long way as the plan does its work.

> Strategic thinking means that you understand what the reactions of teachers will be as you implement the strategic plan *and* that you have a clear idea of what your response will be when they respond to the plan.

LINKING STRATEGIC PLANNING TO BUILDING A LEARNING ORGANIZATION

Intentional and long-range integration of equity and elimination of implicit and explicit bias and structural racism represents perhaps the most challenging work facing educational leaders today. Superintendents and others leading systemic continuous improvement initiatives must understand that strategic planning is always a work in progress, i.e., it is never work that is fully and completely done. For school systems and leaders beginning their antiracism work, strategic planning must emphasize a range of professional learning strategies and processes to promote courageous conversations grounded in objective data, while encouraging honest and challenging discourse among stakeholders and community groups. The process we outlined in Chapter 3 highlights how conversations about race and antiracist work can help forge a consensus on both school and system goals within the planning process. In addition, the strategic planning process—and the information it provides via the key performance indicators and the monitoring process—can be linked to a broader pattern of teacher-led and principal-led inquiry at the school level. By organizing professional learning in support of working toward equity- and antiracism-related key performance indicators (KPIs), school systems can encourage participants to express their personal voice while they unpack the learning and social challenges inherent in the battle to overcome racism and inequity.

Various forms of discourse-based professional learning opportunities might include the key performance indicator results as starting points for professional learning communities and related communities of practice to identify problems of practice extending from inequities in the school system or school. Teachers or others within these professional learning communities can, in turn, formulate a theory of action to develop appropriate classroom-based interventions and use a project management approach to monitoring the progress of goal attainment as measured by KPIs. In this way, the larger strategic planning process might encourage and support other inquiry-focused efforts to address the challenges of racial inequity, perhaps with better results that could be incorporated into the next round of system-wide strategic planning.

KNOW YOUR LIMITS AND KNOW WHAT YOU WANT

Managing change as part of the strategic planning process means that a superintendent or educational leader must understand the change process and realize that it is a long-term endeavor, generally requiring a minimum of five years for full implementation. Leaders need to be sensitive to the inevitable highs and lows associated with the disruption of a traditional system in order to achieve courageous and bold equity and antiracist long-range goals. Many school systems across the United States adopt strategic plans that appear robust and are aesthetically pleasing to the reader; however, the substance and follow-through needed to impact organizational change is nonexistent. Oftentimes, the revolving door of school superintendents and school board members within educational institutions creates the pattern of start and stop efforts to dismantle systemic racism within schools or school systems that stymie educational progress. Even worse, there are school systems without a strategic plan at all.

We also have to stress that backlash in the wake of the attention to systemic racism within US schools has changed the atmosphere surrounding racial justice—even in the time it has taken us to write this book. The attacks on CRT and efforts to stymie reforms that might provide true equity in schools will undoubtedly have a chilling effect on some school system leaders. We believe, however, you can use strategic thinking in the context of the strategic planning process to anticipate reactions that might derail your work and, in effect, head them off.

Recall Figure 3.2 from Chapter 3, "Committing to Equity." In that figure, we showed a triad formed by a commitment to antiracism, racial discomfort, and overt racial animosity. Based on the goals of your strategic plan, think about how you need to engage school board members, community leaders, and parent groups to understand their level of racial discomfort. Racial discomfort in itself is not a barrier to building an antiracist school system. The challenge arises when discomfort morphs into White fragility that then slides into overt racial hostility because the process was not effectively managed. By ensuring that key leaders within the White community, groups of organized parents, students themselves, and teacher unions engage with others who exhibit overt racial hostility, communities can stay anchored in the zone of transformation, rather than be trapped in the zone of opposition. The key element is strategically understanding what will move particular members of the community into the zone of transformation. Your actions will prompt a reaction, but through foresight, communication, and staying committed to the long-range goal of transformation, you can navigate your school system through these challenging waters.

CONCLUSION

Equity-focused educational leaders need to adopt a collaborative and distributed approach to empowering practitioners to be leaders in the continuous improvement process. When the divisions within communities are strong and the rhetoric divisive, it is hard to pursue collaboration and distributed decision-making. When many members of the community are not committed to collaboration—or to racial equity—it seems naïve or foolish to continue to seek collaboration. When this happens, our response is: stick to a strategic planning process that articulates a true sense of your community and your school system's best traits and advance goals and learning objectives that are in keeping with the best spirits of the American experiment in public education. Let the voices of those who have been denied education guide you and work on their behalf. At times, that will require compromise, but it will also require a sense of where Good Trouble lies and why it's good. John Lewis would demand no less of us.

Tips for Engaging Staff in Strategic Planning and Giving Them Voice

6

- Consider how you are making your strategic plan organic and alive as a tool for transformation, rather than an exercise in paper.

- Reflect on what you do as an educational leader to ensure that the school board, administrators, teachers, and support staff understand the strategic planning process and assume responsibility for its outcomes.

- Incorporate your strategic planning goals into your teacher evaluation process to ensure that practices are being implemented in the classroom. For example, emphasize equitable practices in the classroom and provide a rubric that includes specific strategies that can be incorporated into daily instruction.

- Provide executive coaching and professional learning for all leaders to ensure that they are equipped to support staff with implementation of these strategies and practices in the classroom.

Reflective Questions for Implementing Strategic Thinking and Planning

1. **Personal Reflections**

   - As you reflect on your leadership of strategic planning in your school or school system, how might you enhance your plan using the strategies and processes presented in this chapter?

2. **Organizational Insights**

   - How has your school or school system incorporated early warning systems that begin in the elementary school to identify and support underperforming students?
   - To what extent does your strategic plan emphasize the needs and development of the Whole Child, including physical, social-emotional, and academic growth and achievement?

3. **Initial Steps**

   - How will you build consensus about the importance of equity as a driving engine in your strategic planning process?

4. **Long-Range Possibilities**

   - What prior issues and practices have precluded aspects of your strategic plan from being fully operationalized? How can you address those issues to expand your ability to promote equity within your learning organization?
   - How are you ensuring that your school system's strategic planning process is a pre-K–12 initiative in which racial equity is a guiding principle and priority?

5. **Anticipated Barriers and Challenges**

   - How can you help staff to understand the importance of long-range commitment to racial equity within the structure of the strategic planning elements presented in this chapter?

CHAPTER 7

Choose Good Trouble

Be a Bold and Courageous Antiracist School Leader

GUIDING PRINCIPLES

1. Antiracist school leaders boldly and courageously call out practices and policies that are racist and work to dismantle them.
2. Antiracist school leaders find a way to get in the way and cause Good Trouble through vision, integrity, and passion.
3. Antiracist school leaders must accept that this work will be emotionally, physically, and spiritually draining and they must commit to the work anyway.
4. Antiracist school leaders upend established priorities to make racial equity the top priority striving tirelessly for the well-being and academic achievement of BIPOC students.
5. Antiracist school leaders support staff, students, parents, and the community in overcoming adversity and achieving a true vision for equity and the sustained achievement of all learners.

COURAGEOUS AND BOLD LEADERSHIP THROUGH VISION, INTEGRITY, AND PASSION

Leaders solve problems, right? They don't create them. At least, that is the conventional wisdom. But what if solving a problem (racism) means causing other problems (making people in power uncomfortable)? Making explicit the role race plays within schools opens a Pandora's box that is not easily closed. For some people, simply raising the issue of race is a problem itself. From their vantage point, race is something we need to "get over" rather than highlight and focus on.

This view is remarkably common: even Supreme Court Chief Justice John Roberts articulated this view when he wrote in a Supreme Court ruling striking down a voluntary school integration plan: "The way to stop discrimination on the basis of race is to stop discriminating on the basis of race" (*Parents Involved in Community Schools v. Seattle School District*, 2007). In other words, don't talk about it, don't acknowledge it and, by all means, don't see race and act as if it matters. Overcoming this prevailing view takes more than just understanding the history of a school system; it takes leadership. More specifically, it takes bold and courageous leadership.

In this chapter, we turn to the idea of leadership, arguing that boldness and courage are central elements of an antiracist leadership. It takes boldness and courage to name and call out practices and policies that are racist, and doing so, will, inevitably, create "problems." As John Lewis has said, "You must be bold, brave, and courageous and find a way . . . to get in the way." Some will object to your efforts to "stir up trouble." Nonetheless, courageous and bold leadership demands that problems be created, and that difficult and troubling issues about racial equity not be ignored, or placated, but addressed explicitly by students, parents, teachers, school leaders, school board members, civic leaders, and citizens alike.

Our understanding of leadership hinges on two concepts: courage and boldness. In the context of race, those two dimensions of leadership will create problems, precisely because they aim to shift the distribution of opportunities to students. Leadership is the ability to influence, empower, and inspire others to attain a shared goal. An effective leader is one who embodies self-efficacy and truly values the followers they serve. It requires, in short, VIP: vision, integrity, and passion.

Vision allows effective leaders to establish ambitious and attainable goals. Vision is an understanding of one's goals and a clear picture of what the world should look like if your goals are realized. But goals alone are insufficient. An effective leader must also embody personal integrity. The most effective leaders have a moral compass that at all times exudes honesty, transparency, and alignment to their core values. Integrity brings with it the ability to inspire trust, and without trust, no leader will be effective (Bryk & Schneider, 2002; Bryk, 2010). Most importantly, an effective leader must have passion for their work and believe this work fulfills their life's purpose. At their core, a passionate leader can't imagine not undertaking this work; it has become central to their identity.

VIP is not simply a collection of attributes of effective leaders; it maps out how leaders choose to be effective. What unites the elements of VIP is their common focus on longer-term rewards, not quick or easy payoffs. Vision, integrity, and passion act as orienting beacons for work that, at first blush, has few immediate returns. VIP orients and aligns work to tasks that reach beyond the day-to-day and provides perspective to coconspirators, allies, coworkers, and followers that enable them to draw meaning from the courage and boldness of a leader's efforts. Boldness and courage enable a leader to define and articulate a mission; vision, integrity, and passion enable others to share in that mission by orienting and focusing the work. Boldness and courage enable a leader to create good problems, to have the strength to get into Good Trouble at school; vision, integrity, and passion provide the means by which a leader orients the work and inspires others to tackle those good problems with intentionality and eagerness.

THE REALITY OF CAUSING GOOD TROUBLE

There will be costs—deep costs—for engaging in bold and courageous leadership. Let's be clear: being an antiracist leader in the United State is daunting, rare, and comes at a price. Anti-racism challenges the wrongs that have been accepted in our nation for hundreds of years. One must be able and willing to open wounds and scars from the brutal past of our history no matter how painful, emotionally draining, and uncomfortable they may be. Committing a school system to antiracist work is undoubtedly one of the most challenging tasks a school leader could undertake. Leaders working to dismantle systemic racism will face opposition, adversity, controversy, naysayers, and will be confronted by dedicated and skillful opponents who adamantly oppose this work. Knowing one's history—and the history of Good Trouble—we see what has happened in the past to leaders who challenge these systemic injustices.

The cost of causing Good Trouble is real. During the civil rights movement, organized and resourceful opponents to racial justice sought to intimidate, rebuke, and stymie the work of organizations such as the National Association for the Advancement of Colored People (NAACP), the Southern Christian Leadership Conference (SCLC), the Student Non-Violent Coordinating Committee (SNCC), and the Congress of Racial Equality (CORE). Civil rights leaders affiliated with these organizations were ridiculed, defamed, harassed, and assaulted as they fought for equality. Their allies and supporters faced economic pressures as banks called in loans, and employers fired "troublemakers" for expressing their views and fighting for their rights. Some leaders paid the ultimate price: Dr. Martin Luther King, Jr., Medgar Evers, and Malcom X were murdered due to their unapologetic courage and boldness to fight for civil rights and equality.

This is not to say that those who commit to antiracist work will be murdered, but the deaths of these bold and courageous leaders remind us of the deep and persistent hold racism has on all facets of American life. Breaking that hold and preventing its reemergence demands a savvy, persistent, and long-term perspective that is difficult. There is no getting around it: leading a school system to undertake antiracism is some of the hardest work a school leader can do.

The time is now to begin—and extend—this work. The murder of George Floyd at the hands of Minneapolis police, and the murder of Breonna Taylor at the hands of Louisville police, as well as numerous other murders, sparked an uprising that has changed the racial conversation in the United States. Our nation is grappling with what race means in the United States. In that conversation, what was seen previously as audacious and unattainable has now become imaginable and possible. The relentless accumulation of evidence of the ongoing, repressive nature of racism in the United States, seen in police murders of twelve-year-old Tamir Rice and in the vigilante murders of twenty-five-year-old Ahmaud Arbery and fourteen-year-old Trayvon Martin, has shown much of the White community the scope and prevalence of structural racism.

It is simply implausible to deny both the effects and extent of the structural forces of racism arrayed against BIPOC lives. While many in the Black community have long decried the pernicious effects of White supremacy, now Whites must grapple with the reality that not actively opposing racist acts and institutions is to support White supremacy. For Whites, the burden of proof has now shifted: it is no longer enough to vow that they are not racist or discriminatory. Now, a commitment to equity and justice requires one—on an individual and collective level—to become antiracist in order to challenge and confront White supremacy.

We have a once-in-a-generation opportunity to tear down the institutions and practices that sustain White supremacy in schools and to replace them with institutions and practices premised on equity and justice. To not do so is both to squander a moment for justice but also to resign ourselves and our nation to growing disparities, growing inequity, and growing social unrest and decline. Our forefathers and foremothers in this fight—the Fannie Lou Hamers, Ernie Chambers, Ida B. Wells, and Shirley Chisholms—all possessed a fearlessness and boldness to engage the powers that be in a quest for racial justice. The qualities possessed by these fearless leaders must be demonstrated by leaders today who are striving for antiracism. Each of these leaders paid a price for their efforts to make Good Trouble. Likewise, you must be willing to lose friendships or acquaintances, to battle constantly with those opposed to antiracist practices, and unfortunately risk losing your job.

> A commitment to equity and justice requires one—on an individual and collective level—to become antiracist in order to challenge and confront White supremacy.

Antiracist school leaders, particularly after some success in dismantling systemic racism, have been subjected to scrutiny that sometimes leads to their dismissal. They are not fired because their superiors publicly condone racism; instead, they are fired because they "create problems" for some constituency or group as policies and practices shift. When people, typically White people, begin to experience a loss or even the potential loss of privileges that they have had their entire lives, this Good Trouble becomes unsustainable. This is where courage and boldness—guided by vision, integrity, and passion—provides a path forward.

THE OTHER SIDE OF WHITE FRAGILITY

Often a central element of these fights is a reluctance to acknowledge race, or to posit color blindness as the most direct path to equity. For many Whites, especially those whose neighborhoods, communities, or workplaces are populated with only a few people of color, the word "race" makes them uncomfortable and even brings fear. In response, they see color blindness or simply avoiding the question of race, as the most productive path forward. The challenge, of course, is that ignoring race preserves the existing inequities that harms the educational success of students of color. Pushing forward with these conversations and innovations requires a critical mass of White stakeholders to be willing to engage the issue of race. It is that change in perception among White stakeholders that the Black Lives Matter movement has helped foster.

This pressure is even more intense for BIPOC leaders who are actively working to make our nation antiracist. BIPOC leaders must not only overcome adversity but also endure systemic racism personally while trying to dismantle it. African American superintendents in public education comprise only 3 percent of superintendents across the United States; most, if not all, endure racism in their leadership role, on a daily basis—whether through microaggressions, implicit biases, or explicit biases. Many BIPOC leaders encounter these same overt and covert acts of racism throughout their professional careers and personal lives. Fighting, resisting, and transforming these views and actions demand even more passion from BIPOC leaders as they run this marathon of antiracism.

COURAGE AND BOLDNESS CAN REDEFINE PRIORITIES

So what do courage and boldness (guided by vision, integrity, and passion) look like when applied to the daily work of schools? How do we translate the grand rhetoric of civil rights leaders into a to-do list that informs the work of, for lack of a better word, educational bureaucrats? It's one thing for an advocacy organization or a civil rights group to take on the mantle of courage and boldness; it's another for those terms to be woven into the institutional routines of schools and school systems. Committing a school system to an antiracist stance means that courageous and bold leadership is reflected in the routine and daily work of teachers, principals, and school officials at all levels. It means that policies that embody an antiracist perspective guide them in their work, as they make hundreds of decisions in a day about students. These policies not only shape their interactions with students but also have to *reshape* their understanding of how schools, implicitly and explicitly, disadvantage some students and advantage others. These policies need to change the behavior of local administrators and frontline personnel, enabling them to both see how past practices harmed students and to proactively create an antiracist environment. Courage and boldness are necessary but not sufficient attributes of antiracist leadership; they need to be translated into routines and patterns that embody an antiracist commitment and enable it to flourish at all levels.

PLACING RACIAL EQUITY AT THE CENTER IN ALEXANDRIA

One way of doing this is through a direct and explicit declaration that this is the highest priority of the school system. In Alexandria, in the fall of 2019 and into the spring of 2020, we made that declaration through a process that culminated in the adoption of a new strategic plan for the school district. That plan, *ACPS 2025: Equity for All*, which can be found on the school website acps.k12.va.us/2025, placed racial equity at the heart of the work we undertake in the Alexandria City Public Schools (ACPS) (Figure 7.1). This change—seemingly minor from the outside—has the potential to fundamentally transform the priorities by which the school board and school officials design, implement, and evaluate the activities of teachers, principals, coaches, and support staff.

FIGURE 7.1 ● Strategic Plan for Alexandria City Public Schools

IT'S BOLD. IT'S COURAGEOUS.

IT'S ABOUT EQUITY AND EMPOWERMENT AND INSPIRING STUDENTS TO THRIVE

In June 2020, the Alexandria City School Board approved Equity for All 2025, an ambitious strategic plan for Alexandria City Public Schools.

Equity for All 2025 places racial equity at the center of everything that we do as a school division. It challenges us to ensure our students are engaged in classroom instruction and have access to the educational resources needed to enhance their learning experiences. It will ensure that our schools are a safe, friendly and welcoming environment for all. It also sets clear division-wide priorities and programs to address opportunity and achievement gaps as well as makes sure that all students graduate ready for college, careers and life. The vision is big and bold, and the potential is enormous.

Equity for All 2025 has five primary strategic goals. Progress toward these strategic goals will be measured with rigorous metrics. These targets are audacious, but we hope our success will ultimately become a model for urban school divisions around the country.

We are acting with urgency and know that the time is now to educate the next generation. And so, at ACPS, we unapologetically require a standard of excellence for all employees, students and families to ensure that our mission comes to fruition. Success is the only option for the future of ACPS. No matter what other priorities we have going forward, our young people will always be the center of our work, decision-making and mission.

As an urban-suburban school division with a very diverse student population, we are often presented with a unique combination of incredible opportunities and complex challenges. Equity for All 2025 promises to empower all students to thrive in this diverse and ever-changing world so that they can attain their dreams and achieve their own goals.

We are taking action by ensuring that funding, priorities, areas of focus and programs are designed to address barriers to learning regardless of our young people's circumstances. This involves a paradigm shift in our thinking across the school division. It entails a strategic approach to reallocation of human, capital and educational resources to ensure that all students engage in ACPS' educational experiences which will help them thrive in our diverse and ever-changing world.

We cannot do this alone. Equity for All 2025 is part of a bigger unified strategic vision for our city and is aligned with multiple citywide organizations involved in supporting children and families. These organizations, including Alexandria Health Department, Partnership for a Healthier Alexandria and the City of Alexandria's Department of Community and Human Services — responsible for The Children and Youth Master Plan — have partnered in the first unified five-year planning process that will engage and empower the entire city of Alexandria.

Join us in bringing Equity for All 2025 to life, as we work on empowering all our students, helping them to flourish and thrive in whatever college or career pathway they may choose.

GIVE US FIVE FOR 2025.

TABLE OF CONTENTS

Read more about the plan at www.acps.k12.va.us/2025

EQUITY FOR ALL

2025

PARTNERSHIP *for a* HEALTHIER *Alexandria*

Source: Alexandria City Public Schools. (2025). Equity For All: Alexandria City Public Schools Strategic Plan 2020–2025.

Putting racial equity first means that other goals, even long-standing goals that the community has traditionally endorsed, are no longer at the top. That is the true power of an antiracist strategic plan. It reorders priorities; it makes racial equity not simply a nice thing that schools encourage, but the defining characteristic of the education that children receive within a school system. Putting racial equity first is bold and courageous, even if it sounds—on the surface—like yet another flavor-of-the month bureaucratic initiative emanating from the central office.

ACPS 2025: *Equity for All* did more, however, than simply name racial equity as the school system's goal. It articulated a series of steps by which that goal would be realized. The strategic plan begins by identifying an ambitious and attainable mission (empowering all students to thrive in a diverse and ever-changing world), a clear vision (ensuring student success by inspiring students and addressing barriers to learning), and a robust set of core values (ACPS will be welcoming, empowering, equity-focused, innovative, and results driven).

Beyond those broad framing commitments, the strategic plan established a theory of action grounded in, among other things, the beliefs that (1) principals are instructional leaders; (2) the central office exists to support schools, not simply engage in top-down management; (3) decisions and implementation will be the product of foundational principles. To track and evaluate progress, the strategic plan established clear metrics to monitor the school system's progress through an equity dashboard that provides specific data aligned with metrics. For a strategic plan to be effective, leadership needs to explain why its priorities are essential to meeting the needs of the organization, at this moment in time. Similarly, with an antiracist commitment by school system leaders, leadership needs to frankly and clearly articulate the stakes of this commitment.

The dual and intersecting pandemics of 2020—racial injustice and COVID-19—make clear the urgency of the situation for school system leaders. The current crisis of public education—in which schools can no longer provide the direct, material support to students in need, particularly when so few other mechanisms of support for children exist—makes the need for strategic plans like Alexandria's *Equity for All* abundantly clear. Having clear priorities enabled Alexandria to engage in a decision-making process that evaluated pandemic responses in light of racial justice and the needs of our students. When the families of BIPOC students experienced (and are experiencing still) the effects of the pandemic in such unequal ways—disproportionately getting sick and dying from the coronavirus, disproportionately getting laid off from service sector jobs that bear the brunt of economic losses, disproportionately without medical insurance or family resources to carry them through hard times—the strategic plan enabled ACPS to focus intently on the needs of these students and their families. Without racial equity at the core of ACPS's work, defined *prior* to the pandemic and the Black Lives Matter movement, the school system would have been unable to effectively address the needs of *all* of its students.

BOTH SUBSTANCE AND SYMBOLISM MATTER

The mission, vision, and core values of ACPS were tested within the first couple of months of its adoption of *Equity for All*. The school system faced growing calls to change the name of the high school, which was T. C. Williams High School at the time. How could a school system place racial equity at the heart of its work and, at the same time, emblazon the name of a fierce segregationist on its only high school? Members of the Black community in Alexandria had petitioned to change the name of the school as early as the late 1960s. Unfortunately, the success of the 1971 state championship football team, immortalized in the movie *Remember the Titans*, ironically made changing the name of the now world-famous T. C. Williams High School a heavier lift.

Nonetheless, in the late spring and early summer of 2020, as the Black Lives Matter movement brought forward an uprising of protests, members of the Alexandria community began rallying once again to change the name—and to change it immediately. Petitions circulated, news stories were aired, students placed a tarp over the school's marquee, and community support to change the name swelled. As a politically liberal community, Alexandria, in large part, supported the activism and protests of the Black Lives Matter movement. Many members of the community, alumni, and current students who sought an immediate change in the name of Alexandria's high school were White. They insisted that the name of the high school was an affront to students of color and the school district should immediately distance itself from the name of a segregationist.

Many within the school system and city's leadership circle supported the name change, committed to the belief that all students (BIPOC or not) should not be subject to overt racism each day by attending a school that was intentionally named for a man who publicly opposed the inclusion of BIPOC students in ACPS. What was being left out of the conversation, a conversation often led by White advocates, were the actual voices of BIPOC students, especially those at T. C. Williams High School. It became obvious that changing the name quickly, without addressing the underlying issue—the continuing inequitable outcomes among students where White students were privileged above BIPOC students—would not be an adequate solution and would have been an enormous lost opportunity.

The central tension in the rush to change the name was an all-too-common problem as White people took up the banner of racial justice: focusing on the alleviation of White guilt or complicity rather than focusing on the inequity in power that racist policies generate and sustain. Most White supporters of the name change saw themselves as allies of the movement for racial justice, particularly in the intense months after the murder of George Floyd. That allyship is important and essential (particularly as it empowers White people to engage other White people on racist beliefs and practices) (Campt, 2018), but that allyship can also allow current inequities of power to privileged White voices over the voices of BIPOC students and Black community members.

> An all-too-common problem as White people took up the banner of racial justice: focusing on the alleviation of White guilt or complicity rather than focusing on the inequity in power that racist policies generate and sustain.

When that happens, White allyship tips into something else: a stance that allows some White people to feel atoned for the wrongs of our horrific history with regards to BIPOC in the United States. That very stance, however, prevents the community from recognizing and working toward the dismantling of policies that generate racial inequity in the first place. Some White people believe that stating "Black Lives Matter" or sharing the personal stories of BIPOC students is enough; in reality, that check-the-box commitment to racial justice prevents us from advancing the harder and more difficult work of dismantling systemic racism.

As the emails flooded in and the public pleas arose from many White people in Alexandria (claiming to speak on behalf of BIPOC students despite their minimal interaction with or understanding of BIPOC students), we decided to be methodical and strategic and not rush the name change process. We wanted to be intentional, even instructional, and connect the name to practices, both in the past and in the present. That move toward being methodical, strategic, and reflective took courage and boldness because it moved beyond the superficial and connected Thomas Chambliss Williams the man to T.C. Williams the school—both past and present.

The commitment to disrupt the existing power dynamics challenged the existing array of White privilege that exists within ACPS—and thousands of other school systems like it. This privilege empowers parents, students, and administrators and community members who have long taken for granted their ability to set the agenda for both the schools and the community. This disruption takes far more courage than swapping one name for another.

Our first step in this more intentional process was to step back and allow high school students, specifically BIPOC high school students, to lead the efforts and educate the community on the raw, horrific, and unfiltered history of ACPS and the city of Alexandria. In an educational climate in which students rarely have power to set the curricular agenda or the agendas of policymakers, it took courage and boldness to explicitly empower BIPOC high school students to express their truth. Josefina Owusu, president of the Black Students Union at T. C., told Hannah Natanson of the *Washington Post*, "Having to go to a school named for someone who doesn't see you as human is unbearable." She added that "For students of color, to chant his name at pep rallies or on the field is to embrace a racist culture that stems from the oppression of African Americans for more than 400 years" (Natanson, 2020).

This leadership from youth activists inspired many within the community as they unapologetically related their experiences of attending a school named after a segregationist as well as exposed the ugly truth of the school system's racist history. Other students, meanwhile, took exception to the argument that the 1971 football championship—and the film *Remember the Titans*—had immortalized the name T. C. Williams. For many students, the film was as much a part of the past as the championship and T. C. Williams himself: Anais Joubert, a fourteen-year-old ninth grader told the *Post*, "Yeah, sure, it was a big thing, there was a movie, but the movie is really old now, and our generation doesn't really care about the movie. . . . It's a serious disservice to the actual students now, to privilege your nostalgia" (Natanson, 2020).

Empowering Antiracist Student Leaders

Alexandria, Virginia

The two student school board representatives (who happened to be BIPOC students) led student discussions on the history of the Alexandria City Public Schools and organized community engagement among student organizations to increase awareness of T. C. Williams's past and an understanding of its connection to the present.

Empowering Antiracist Community Leaders

Alexandria, Virginia

With students leading the conversations within schools, ACPS also reached out to the community, holding community read-ins that engaged and recounted unflattering historical moments that were the precursor to the racial inequities that still permeated the school division in 2020. The community read-ins were facilitated by school board members, students, ACPS staff, and community leaders, enabling a broader set of actors to both discover and share the historical contexts of Alexandria's racial journey. Book studies and reading circles on two books (*Building the Federal Schoolhouse* by Dr. Douglas Reed (2014) and *How to Be an Antiracist* by Dr. Ibram X. Kendi (2019)) were conducted to build an understanding of the historical context and to establish a foundation for the work to become an antiracist school system that lies ahead. People of color, especially African Americans, in the city of Alexandria have advocated for a renaming since the school opened in 1965. This was an opportunity to ensure that their advocacy and voices were not in vain; we sought to honor the many civil rights leaders within the city of Alexandria by connecting the next generation of leaders to the courage and boldness of leaders who paved their way.

One of the challenges as this conversation unfolded was the rejoinder that this revisiting of the past was counterproductive, that it was too focused on a past that everyone rejected and readily acknowledged. "Why belabor the point that T. C. Williams was a segregationist?" some contended. "We all have moved beyond those days. Telling and retelling that history will just renew grudges and make it harder for us all to move forward together." This argument—in effect, to let bygones be bygones—ignores and discounts an important element of antiracist work: by telling the stories, and hearing the stories, we as a community validate and legitimize the current claims for racial justice. These stories teach us that our history is not over, is not dead and buried. It lives on—and as Donald Trump's campaign against critical race theory shows—it is sustained precisely because it is not acknowledged and confronted, as both a history lived through and a present we are creating.

In the midst of a pandemic and global protests over racial injustice, the call to rename a school is both a small and a large event. It is small in the sense that one school, in one community, does not represent a wholesale transformation of the racial order in the United States. It is a large event, however, when those demands to change a name are fused to an understanding of why that name was originally chosen—to reward a segregationist for his decades-long work in creating and sustaining racial inequality in public education—and how that name connects to the daily practices of racial inequity that still structure and shape public education in the United States. Getting from small to large required ACPS to be methodical and strategic as well as to reflect and to learn those lessons of the past and present. Only by a thoughtful, intentional, and educative understanding of the true meaning of a name could the community embark on a process that undoes the effects of that name. The Alexandria City School Board unanimously renamed T. C. Williams High School to Alexandria City High School in November 2020.

Letting bygones be bygones ignores and discounts an important element of antiracist work: by telling the stories, and hearing the stories, we as a community validate and legitimate the current claims for racial justice.

THE VISION FORWARD: THE CONNECTED HIGH SCHOOL NETWORK

While much of the discussion surrounding the name change of Alexandria's only high school revolved around the community's past and present, the challenge of the future has also presented itself with urgency and complexity. Alexandria has had only one high school since 1971, a source of civic cohesion even as the city has grown and become more racially complex and multicultural. While the Black–White dichotomy still defines much of Alexandria's racial dynamics, the city's increasing immigration, its growing population of English learners, and the influx of students from disparate places and cultures across the globe have made Alexandria's single high school a very complex place. It is also a very crowded space, with an expanding student body exceeding the building's original capacity. The original T. C. Williams High School, which opened in 1965, was replaced in 2008, increasing the square footage significantly. Even with that expansion, the new T. C. building quickly became overcrowded as enrollments grew. Between 2008 and 2020, in which one generation of students moved through a PreK–12 system, ACPS's enrollment grew by 25 percent.

Today, Alexandria City High School is one of the largest high schools in the country with 4,000 students enrolled in grades nine through twelve and a projected enrollment of over 5,000 students as soon as 2025. Ensuring that students could form bonds with teachers and staff, as well as each other, in such a large school is an enormous challenge. Part of the solution has been to house ninth graders in a separate building, in which small learning communities can help students make the transition to high school. But even with the Minnie Howard campus in operation, the overcrowding—and the imminent prospect of more student growth—required the district to take action.

The usual response in this scenario would be to seek funding from the community to build a new high school in response to increasing enrollment. In a well-funded and supportive community like Alexandria, that conventional choice would have, no doubt, produced a lovely building full of 21st century amenities designed to engage student learning and development. The problem, however, is that a second high school, with traditional geographically defined attendance zones, would perpetuate the educational racial divide within a city that is already racially and economically divided by neighborhoods. The existing high school in Alexandria already had systemic racism within its brick and mortar, providing BIPOC students an educational experience that differs substantially from their White counterparts.

Through course selections, clubs, and sports, White students and BIPOC students move, seemingly, through two different high schools located within the same space. The creation of two physically separate high schools would, we feared, quickly become, through housing shifts and demographic realignment in the city, racially identified and would only exacerbate the existing educational inequities within Alexandria. So, instead of perpetuating systemic racism, the school division made a courageous and bold move to keep one high school within the city of Alexandria and developed the concept of the Connected High School Network (CHSN) (Figure 7.2).

CHSN is a courageous and bold endeavor to prevent the school system from entrenching race and class divisions in its secondary schools, as it seeks to create the space to teach students. The goal of CHSN is to afford all students equity, access, and engagement regardless of their race or socioeconomics. On the one hand, the idea is simple: students, utilizing experiential learning opportunities within the community, rotate through learning experiences at multiple sites, but with Alexandria's single high school as their primary base of operations. The satellite campuses house the community

Connected High School Network Concept

Expanded with Specialty Learning Centers

Primary Campus
Capacity ~2,900

Specialty Learning Center
Capacity 400-600

Specialty Learning Center
Capacity 400-600

Specialty Learning Center
Capacity 400-600

Specialty Learning Center
Capacity 400-600

○ Primary Campus

● Specialty Learning Centers
- Purpose-built or long-term lease buildings
- Hosts multiple affinity programs (thematic)
- Division-provided transport
- Half- or full-day sessions

EXAMPLES of Discrete Off-site Programs
- Shared or leased space
- Pop-up programs (temporary)
- Accommodates demand
- Existing examples include Chance for Change and Satellite Campus

EXAMPLES of Individual Field Studies
- Internships
- Professional cadets
- Project-partnerships
- Apprenticeships
- Service learning
- Work study

ACPS Alexandria City Public Schools   Stantec   fmi

Source: Alexandria City Public Schools. (2018). The High School Project: Inspiring a Future for Alexandria—School Board Workshop Session: Discover + Engage.

partnerships and experiential opportunities and operate as learning labs for students, thereby reducing the daily attendance load at the main high school building. The plan is ambitious, even audacious, and the administrative and curricular undertaking required to pull this off is complex, even daunting.

Educational design teams, working with industry advisory boards, must design curricula along multiple themes that are aligned with state standards and draw on community resources. For example, a STEM (science, technology, engineering, and mathematics) industry advisory board, in conjunction with the educational design team, designed modules, curricula, and learning experiences within multiple areas, ranging from architecture and construction, health science, information technology, manufacturing, and green energy. Other curricular areas in which ACPS developed experiential learning modules include The Arts, Education and Human Services, and Business and Government. In addition, the school system drew on an existing Early College program (in conjunction with Northern Virginia Community College) and the incoming Virginia Tech Innovation Campus (which is partnering with Amazon at HQ2, its new Northern Virginia second headquarters site) to offer experiential learning and advanced learning opportunities simply unavailable within a conventional high school.

As transformative as this new vision of high school may be, it also holds risks—for both the school system and students. As students make decisions about which programs, if any, they want to pursue at the satellite campuses, they could be tracked, as they have in the past, into less demanding courses or programs or could opt for a course study that will not meet their long-term needs.

The CHSN is based on academic research (McDonald et al., 2009) and will have a positive impact on academic achievement—including improving achievement for subgroups—and the positive impact on interpersonal, social, and emotional skills. This approach ensures that students can show they have learned to think critically, creatively, and collaboratively and communicate well. Students also will be able to display academic and technical knowledge, demonstrate workplace skills and behaviors, build connections in their communities, show responsibility, and align their personal skills, knowledge, and interests with some career goals within a diverse school environment through this innovative approach. Most of all, this approach, by ensuring that all students have a seat in

Alexandria's single high school, will prevent the de facto resegregation of secondary schooling in Alexandria.

CONCLUSION

Courage and boldness are not simply rhetorical exertions designed to fire your team with enthusiasm. They are central elements of your strategic plan to build an antiracist school system. Without courage and boldness, you will not have the momentum to engage what are deeply engrained and embedded practices in US schooling. The need to rethink and reconceptualize our institutions of schooling to ensure equity demands a courage to challenge existing forces and a boldness to think on a transformative scale. Leaders of the civil rights movement—of today and yesterday—do not accept modest and incremental change; nor should the leaders of our educational systems. Without courage and boldness, we will simply replicate the existing plagues of inequity and discrimination.

Tips for Being a Bold and Courageous Antiracist School Leader

7

1. Make racial equity your first priority—the defining characteristic of the education that children receive in your school system.

2. Have the courage to open wounds and scars from the brutal past of history no matter how painful, emotionally draining, and uncomfortable they may be.

3. Be prepared to face opposition, adversity, controversy, naysayers, and to be confronted by dedicated and skillful opponents who adamantly oppose the work of racial equity.

4. Understand that not actively opposing racist acts and institutions is to support White supremacy.

5. Tear down the institutions and practices that sustain White supremacy in schools and replace them with institutions and practices premised on equity and justice.

6. Empower BIPOC students to fully participate in your efforts toward racial equity.

Reflective Questions for Being a Bold and Courageous Antiracist School Leader

1. **Personal Reflections**

   - What are examples of when you have demonstrated courage and boldness in your career as an educator and leader?

2. **Organizational Insights**

   - How can professional learning and strategic planning reinforce systemic efforts to reduce or eliminate inequities and imbalances within your school system?
   - To what extent can educational leaders support and reinforce students' and staff's sense of self-efficacy and engagement as part of the equity agenda?

3. **Initial Steps**

   - What data are available to help you identify areas in which systemic racism and related inequities require immediate attention and action for BIPOC?

4. **Long-Range Possibilities**

   - How will you monitor the long-term impact of strategic changes you are supporting to eliminate the impact of systemic racism, implicit/explicit bias, and disproportionality?

5. **Anticipated Barriers and Challenges**

   - What challenges and resistance do you anticipate—or have you already observed—as you implement an equity agenda in your school or school system?
   - How can you work with others to identify and help all stakeholders be conscious of the long-term negative impact of racial inequities, academic disparities, and historical oppression in your school or school system?

CHAPTER 8

Conclusion

You've made it to the end of our book. We hope that you are just as proud as we are with your intentional efforts to become an antiracist school leader. We recognize that the challenge is daunting, but we hope we have provided you with deeper knowledge, actionable steps, and a bit of inspiration as you undertake this work. We haven't sugarcoated anything or made simplistic promises, but we are convinced—based on the research and our own experience—that the components that we have laid out here will spark remarkable changes in your school or school system and, with persistence, throughout our nation. Knowing your history and telling your school's or school system's counter-narratives; committing yourself, your staff, and your teachers fully to equity; working to reduce and eliminate tracking; making your school's disciplinary practices formative not punitive; engaging in strategic thinking and planning for equity; and, importantly being bold and courageous—these are the prerequisites for building a school system that does not simply tolerate the presence of BIPOC students but which will finally fulfill the promise of democratic equality that public schools have long claimed to be central to their mission.

We ask that you use this book not as a full repository of everything you need to do within your school system but as a starting point and a launching pad for the continued learning, exploration, and mastery you will need to address racism in our schools. This book is something of a toolkit. Like most books on education, it has facts, data, and knowledge that you consume and, in turn, learn from. But it is our hope that the book also serves as a way to puzzle you, to posit challenging and complex questions for which there are no right or easy answers. We've woven those tools throughout the book. If you haven't stopped and explored the *Guiding Principles* at the beginning of each chapter and the *Reflective Questions* at the end, we ask that you go back and re-engage those sections of the texts. They are not simply aids to help you learn, they are also confounding and challenging problems and tasks and you will need much practice before you implement your strategic plan for your school system.

As you continue on your bold and courageous journey toward antiracism, it is imperative that you utilize the extensive resources available to help you and your team navigate these uncharted waters. We provided the Guiding Principles and Reflective Questions with the conviction that achieving equity in schools begins with a clear understanding of the contexts of schooling as well as concrete and actionable steps that parents, teachers, students, principals, administrators, and school system leaders can take in their daily work with schools. This is a book for both understanding and action. It is intended to serve as a guide for your courageous and bold journey to becoming an antiracist school system. As you work tirelessly to ensure that all students—especially BIPOC students—receive the education to which they are entitled, it is essential for you to build your understanding at the same time you build your professional capacity to make Good Trouble.

Appendix

RESOURCES TO HELP YOU ON YOUR ANTIRACIST JOURNEY

We would like to provide you with resources that may be helpful to you and your team as you begin your antiracism journey. We hope you will utilize these resources to expand your knowledge. They are by no means the only way to attain your goal of becoming an antiracist school system—they are just the golden nuggets that we've found helpful to us on our own journey.

Chapter 1: Supplemental Resources for Getting Into Good Trouble

The Annie E. Casey Foundation

The Annie E. Casey Foundation (AECF) is devoted to developing a brighter future for millions of children at risk of poor educational, economic, social, and health outcomes.

https://www.aecf.org/blog/racial-justice-definitions

The BIPOC Project

The BIPOC Project aims to build authentic and lasting solidarity among Black, Indigenous, and People of Color (BIPOC), in order to undo Native invisibility, anti-Blackness, dismantle White supremacy, and advance racial justice.

https://www.thebipocproject.org/

The William and Flora Hewlett Foundation

The William and Flora Hewlett Foundation is a nonpartisan, private charitable foundation that advances ideas and supports institutions to promote a better world.

https://hewlett.org/our-approach-to-systemic-racism-in-open-education/

Usable Knowledge

Usable Knowledge was founded to connect research to practice. The organization seeks to make education research and well-vetted strategies accessible to a wide audience: teachers and principals, district leaders, policymakers, university faculty and higher ed professionals, nonprofit leaders, entrepreneurs, members of the media, and parents.

https://www.gse.harvard.edu/news/uk/18/02/exploring-ethnic-racial-identity

Chapter 2: Supplemental Resources for Knowing Your History to Rewrite Your Future

The Center for Intercultural Dialogue

The Center for Intercultural Dialogue operates under the auspices of the Council of Communication Associations (Washington, DC). The Council of Communication Associations (CCA) is an umbrella organization for seven national and international communication associations based in the United States.

https://centerforinterculturaldialogue.files.wordpress.com/2014/10/key-concept-counter-narrative.pdf

Organization of American Historians (OAH)

Founded in 1907, the Organization of American Historians (OAH) is the largest professional society dedicated to the teaching and study of American history. The mission of the organization is to promote excellence in the scholarship, teaching, and presentation of American history, and to encourage wide discussion of historical questions and the equitable treatment of all practitioners of history.

https://www.oah.org/tah/issues/2017/february/the-troubled-history-of-american-education-after-the-brown-decision/

The Education Trust

The Education Trust is a national nonprofit that works to close opportunity gaps that disproportionately affect students of color and students from low-income families. Through research and advocacy, Ed Trust supports efforts that expand excellence and equity in education from preschool through college, increase college access and completion particularly for historically underserved students, engage diverse communities dedicated to education equity, and increase political and public will to act on equity issues.

https://edtrust.org/wp-content/uploads/2014/09/Core-Equity-Narrative-Presentation-Updated-12-04-2017.pdf

The Southern Regional Education Board (SREB)

The Southern Regional Education Board works with states to improve public education at every level, from early childhood through doctoral education. SREB helps policymakers make informed decisions by providing independent, accurate data and recommendations. SREB helps educators strengthen student learning with professional development, proven practices, and curricula.

https://www.sreb.org/sites/main/files/file-attachments/20v08_inequity_in_education_report.pdf?1602247064

Chapter 3: Supplemental Resources for Committing to Racial Equity

The Learning Policy Institute

The Learning Policy Institute conducts and communicates independent, high-quality research to improve education policy and practice. Working with policymakers, researchers, educators, community groups, and others the Institute seeks to advance evidence-based policies that support empowering and equitable learning for each and every child. Nonprofit and nonpartisan, the Institute connects policymakers and stakeholders at the local, state, and federal levels with the evidence, ideas, and actions needed to strengthen the education system from preschool through college and career readiness.

https://learningpolicyinstitute.org/product/advancing-education-2020-brief

United States Department of Education (USDOE)

The USDOE mission is to promote student achievement and preparation for global competitiveness by fostering educational excellence and ensuring equal access.

https://www2.ed.gov/about/offices/list/oese/oss/technical assistance/educatorequity.html

American Institutes for Research (AIR)

AIR is one of the world's largest behavioral and social science research and evaluation organizations. Their overriding goal is to use the best science available to bring the most effective ideas and approaches to enhancing everyday life. AIR believes that making the world a better place is not wishful thinking.

https://www.air.org/topic/education/equity-education

The Intercultural Development Research Association (IDRA)

The Intercultural Development Research Association (IDRA) is an independent, nonprofit organization. Their mission is to achieve equal educational opportunity for every child through strong public schools that prepare all students to access and succeed in college. IDRA strengthens and transforms public education by providing dynamic training; useful research, evaluation, and frameworks for action; timely policy analyses; and innovative materials and programs.

https://www.idra.org/change-model/quality-schools-action-framework/

The Urban Institute

Committed to equity, anchored in data, the Urban Institute advances some of the most rigorous research into the structure of educational opportunity in the United States. As an independent research organization, it allows its researchers to follow their data and analysis without partisan favor. At the same time, they structure diversity into the foundations of their research projects and investigations and see policy issues holistically, connecting education, housing, poverty, health, and human capital.

https://www.urban.org/

Chapter 4: Supplemental Resources for Dismantling Tracking and Within-School Segregation

PDK, International

Established in 1906, PDK International supports teachers and school leaders by strengthening their interest in the profession through the entire arc of their career.

https://kappanonline.org/korbey-russo-covering-gifted-programs-through-an-equity-lens/

The Hunt Institute

The Hunt Institute brings together people and resources to inspire and inform elected officials and policymakers about key issues in education, resulting in visionary leaders who are prepared to take strategic action for greater educational outcomes and student success.

https://hunt-institute.org/wp-content/uploads/2021/02/HI-Duke-Brief-Stephens.pdf

The Brookings Institution

The Brookings Institution is a nonprofit public policy organization based in Washington, DC. Their mission is to conduct in-depth research that leads to new ideas for solving problems facing society at the local, national, and global level.

https://www.brookings.edu/research/the-resurgence-of-ability-grouping-and-persistence-of-tracking/

Facing History

Facing History and Ourselves uses lessons of history to challenge teachers and their students to stand up to bigotry and hate.

https://www.facinghistory.org/educator-resources/current-events/persistence-racial-segregation-american-schools#

Chapter 5: Supplemental Resources for Making School Discipline Different From Policing

Positive Behavioral Interventions and Supports (PBIS)

The OSEP Technical Assistance Center on Positive Behavioral Interventions and Supports (PBIS) was initially funded in 1998. In October 2018, a new five-year funding cycle was launched. The purpose of the new center is to improve the capacity of state education agencies (SEAs), local education agencies (LEAs), and schools to establish, scale up, and sustain the PBIS framework to (a) scale up Tier 2 and 3 systems to improve outcomes for students with or at-risk for disabilities, (b) enhance school climate and school safety, and (c) improve conditions for learning to promote the well-being of all students.

https://www.pbis.org/pbis/getting-started

The International Institute for Restorative Practices (IIRP) Graduate School

The International Institute for Restorative Practices (IIRP) Graduate School was established to advance restorative practices, the science of relationships, and community. They offer advanced master's degrees and graduate certificates to dedicated individuals who believe healthy relationships are the key to continual improvement in their professional environment.

https://www.iirp.edu/restorative-practices/what-is-restorative-practices

The Schott Foundation

The Schott Foundation is a national public fund serving as a bridge between philanthropic partners and advocates to build movements to provide all students an opportunity to learn.

http://schottfoundation.org/restorative-practices

The ACLU

The American Civil Liberties Union (ACLU) dares to create a more perfect union—beyond one person, party, or side. Its mission is to realize this promise of the US Constitution for all and expand the reach of its guarantees.

https://www.aclu.org/issues/juvenile-justice/school-prison-pipeline

Chapter 6: Supplemental Resources for Implementing Strategic Thinking and Planning

The Public Education Leadership Project (PELP)

The Public Education Leadership Project (PELP) aims to increase its intellectual contribution to the field through expanded partnerships among Harvard faculty, doctoral students, and the field. With its core focus on strategic decision making in large urban school systems, PELP offers an extraordinary opportunity to develop new knowledge that extends Harvard's intellectual contribution to the field across schools and disciplines, expands the connection to useful knowledge by its doctoral programs and students, and influences the work of the largest school systems in the country, with implications for public education as a whole.

https://pelp.fas.harvard.edu/coherence-framework#

The Aspen Institute

The Aspen Institute has earned a reputation for gathering diverse, nonpartisan thought leaders, creatives, scholars, and members of the public to address some of the world's most complex problems. But the goal of these convenings is to have an impact beyond the conference room. They are designed to provoke, further, and improve actions taken in the real world.

https://www.wallacefoundation.org/knowledge-center/Documents/Theory-of-Change-Tool-for-Strategic-Planning-Report-on-Early-Experiences.pdf

The Government Alliance on Race and Equity (GARE)

The Government Alliance on Race and Equity (GARE) is a national network of government working to achieve racial equity and advance opportunities for all. The Alliance is a joint project of the new Race Forward and the Othering and Belonging Institute.

https://www.racialequityalliance.org/wp-content/uploads/2016/11/GARE-Racial-Equity-Action-Plans.pdf

Chapter 7: Supplemental Resources for Being a Bold and Courageous Antiracist School Leader

VeryWell Mind

For more than twenty years, the VeryWell Mind worked hard to create and refine a curated library of comprehensive and trustworthy information. A team of writers and editors who are industry experts, including health care professionals and health journalists, who write and continually update a 5,500+ article library.

https://www.verywellmind.com/status-quo-bias-psychological-definition-4065385

Project Implicit

Project Implicit is a nonprofit organization and international collaboration between researchers who are interested in implicit social cognition—thoughts and feelings outside of conscious awareness and control. The goal of the organization is to educate the public about hidden biases and to provide a "virtual laboratory" for collecting data on the Internet.

https://implicit.harvard.edu/implicit/takeatouchtest.html

United Negro College Fund (UNCF)

UNCF's mission is to build a robust and nationally recognized pipeline of underrepresented students who, because of UNCF support, become highly qualified college graduates and to ensure that our network of member institutions is a respected model of best practice in moving students to and through college.

https://uncf.org/pages/k-12-disparity-facts-and-stats

References

Adelman, C. (2006). *The toolbox revisited: Paths to degree completion from high school through college*. US Department of Education.

American Psychological Association Zero Tolerance Task Force. (2008). Are zero tolerance policies effective in the schools? An evidentiary review and recommendations. *The American Psychologist, 63*(9), 852–862.

Ball, M. S. (1990). The legal academy and minority scholars. *Harvard Law Review, 103*(8), 1855–1863.

Brown v. Board of Education of Topeka, 347 U.S. 483 (1954).

Bryk, A. S. (2010). Organizing schools for improvement. *Phi Delta Kappan, 91*(7), 23–30.

Bryk, A., & Schneider, B. (2002). *Trust in schools: A core resource for improvement*. Russell Sage Foundation.

Campt, D. W. (2018). *The White ally toolkit workbook: Using active listening, empathy, and personal storytelling to promote racial equity*. I AM Publications.

Chetty, R., Stepner, M., Abraham, S., Lin, S., Scuderi, B., Turner, N., ... Cutler, D. (2016). The association between income and life expectancy in the United States, 2001–2014. *JAMA, 315*(16), 1750–1766.

Chu, E. M., & Ready, D. D. (2018). Exclusion and urban public high schools: Short- and long-term consequences of school suspensions. *American Journal of Education, 124*(4), 479–509.

Coates, T. N. (2015). *Between the world and me*. Text publishing.

Davis, F. (2018). Whole school restorative justice as a racial justice and liberatory practice: Oakland's journey. *Int'l J. Restorative Just., 1*, 428.

Day, J. C. (2020). Black High School Attainment Nearly on Par With National Average. *America Counts*. https://www.census.gov/library/stories/2020/06/black-high-school-attainment-nearly-on-par-with-national-average.html

Delgado, R. (1989). Storytelling for oppositionists and others: A plea for narrative. *Michigan Law Review, 87*, 2411.

Dewey, J. (1923). *Democracy and education: An introduction to the philosophy of education*. Macmillan.

DiAngelo, R. (2018). *White fragility: Why it's so hard for White people to talk about racism*. Beacon Press.

Digest of Educational Statistics, U. D. o. E. (2018). *Table 219.46. Public high school 4-year adjusted cohort graduation rate (ACGR), by selected student characteristics and state: 2010–11 through 2017–18*. https://nces.ed.gov/programs/digest/d19/tables/dt19_219.46.asp

Digest of Educational Statistics, U. D. o. E. (2018). *Table E. Median annual earnings of full-time year-round workers 25 years old and over, by selected levels of educational attainment and sex: Selected years, 1995 through 2017*. https://nces.ed.gov/pubs2020/2020009.pdf

DiIulio, J. J. (1995, November 27). *The coming of the super–predators*. The Weekly Standard. https://advance-lexis-com.proxy.library.georgetown.edu/api/document?collection=news&id=urn:contentItem:3S3V-26B0-00CY-N3RX-00000-00&context=1516831

Duckworth, A. (2018). *Grit: The power of passion and perseverance* (First Scribner trade paperback edition. ed.). Scribner.

Duncan, G. J., & Murnane, R. J. (2011). *Whither opportunity?: Rising inequality, schools, and children's life chances*. Russell Sage Foundation.

Ewing, E. L. (2018). *Ghosts in the schoolyard: Racism and school closings on Chicago's South Side*. University of Chicago Press.

Felitti, V. J., Anda, R. F., Nordenberg, D., Williamson, D. F., Spitz, A. M., Edwards, V., & Marks, J. S. (1998). Relationship of childhood abuse and household dysfunction to many of the leading causes of death in adults: The Adverse Childhood Experiences (ACE) study. *American Journal of Preventive Medicine*, 14(4), 245–258.

Fryer Jr., R. G., & Levitt, S. D. (2004). Understanding the Black-White test score gap in the first two years of school. *Review of Economics and Statistics*, 86(2), 447–464.

Fryer Jr., R. G., & Levitt, S. D. (2006). The Black-White test score gap through third grade. *American Law and Economics Review*, 8(2), 249–281.

Gamoran, A. (2009). Tracking and inequality: New directions for research and practice. WCER *Working Paper No. 2009-6*. Wisconsin Center for Education Research (NJ1).

González, N., Moll, L. C., & Amanti, C. (2006). *Funds of knowledge: Theorizing practices in households, communities, and classrooms*. Routledge.

Gregory, A., Skiba, R. J., & Noguera, P. A. (2010). The achievement gap and the discipline gap: Two sides of the same coin? *Educational Researcher*, 39(1), 59–68.

Hammond, Z. (2014). *Culturally responsive teaching and the brain: Promoting authentic engagement and rigor among culturally and linguistically diverse students*. Corwin.

Hernandez, D. J. (2011). Double jeopardy: How third-grade reading skills and poverty influence high school graduation. Annie E. Casey Foundation.

Homer, E. M., & Fisher, B. W. (2020). Police in schools and student arrest rates across the United States: Examining differences by race, ethnicity, and gender. *Journal of School Violence*, 19(2), 192–204.

Hwang, N. (2018). Suspensions and achievement: Varying links by type, frequency, and subgroup. *Educational Researcher*, 47(6), 363–374.

Ingersoll, R. M., May, H., & Collins, G. (2019). Recruitment, employment, retention and the minority teacher shortage. *Education Policy Analysis Archives*, 27(37).

Kang-Brown, J., Trone, J., Fratello, J., & Daftary-Kapur, T. (2013). *A generation later: What we've learned about zero tolerance in schools*. Vera Institute of Justice, Center of Youth Justice.

Kendi, I. X. (2019). *How to be an antiracist*. One world.

King Jr., M. L. (1967). *After civil rights: Black power* [Interview]. National Broadcasting Company. https://www.nbcnews.com/video/martin-luther-king-jr-speaks-with-nbc-news-11-months-before-assassination-1202163779741

Kolluri, S. (2018). Advanced Placement: The dual challenge of equal access and effectiveness. *Review of Educational Research*, 88(5), 671–711.

Lee, T., Cornell, D., Gregory, A., & Fan, X. (2011). High suspension schools and dropout rates for Black and White students. *Education and Treatment of Children*, 167–192.

Legette, K. (2018). School tracking and youth self-perceptions: Implications for academic and racial identity. *Child Development*, 89(4), 1311–327.

Lesnick, J., George, R., Smithgall, C., & Gwynne, J. (2010). Reading on grade level in third grade: How is it related to high school performance and college enrollment? Chicago, IL: Chapin Hall at the University of Chicago, 1, 12.

Levin, H. M. (1990). At-risk students in a yuppie age. *Educational Policy*, 4(4), 283–295.

Loveless, T. (2013). *How well are American students learning? The 2013 Brown Center report on American education*. Brookings Institution: Washington (DC), USA.

Mabee, C. (1968). A Negro boycott to integrate Boston schools. *The New England Quarterly*, 41(3), 341–361.

McDonald, J. P., Klein, E. J., & Riordan, M. (2009). *Going to scale with new school designs: Reinventing high school. The series on school reform*. ERIC.

Monahan, K. C., VanDerhei, S., Bechtold, J., & Cauffman, E. (2014). From the school yard to the squad car: School discipline, truancy, and arrest. *Journal of Youth and Adolescence*, 43(7), 1110–1122.

Morris, E. W., & Perry, B. L. (2016). The punishment gap: School suspension and racial disparities in achievement. *Social Problems*, 63(1), 68–86.

N. A. A. C. P. (1954, May 18). Sets advanced goals: Officials say they will drive for end of residential and job discrimination. *New York Times*. https://www-proquest-com.proxy.library.georgetown.edu/historical-newspapers/n-c-p-sets-advanced-goals/docview/112916156/se-2?accountid=11091

Natanson, H. (2020). History meets mythology: Debate stirs over push to rename T.C. Williams High School, of 'Remember the Titans' fame: The school's namesake, Thomas Chambliss Williams, advocated segregation and argued Black and White students learn differently. *The Washington Post (Online)*.

National Assessment of Educational Progress. (2019). *In Chart generated from NAEP data explorer*.

Oakes, J. (2005). *Keeping track: How schools structure inequality*. Yale University Press.

Office of Civil Rights, U. S. D. o. E. (2012). *The transformed Civil Rights Data Collection (CRDC)*. https://www2.ed.gov/about/offices/list/ocr/docs/crdc-2012-data-summary.pdf

Office of Retirement Policy, S. S. A. (2015). *Research summary: Education and lifetime earnings*. Washington, DC.

Paradies, Y. (2006). A systematic review of empirical research on self-reported racism and health. *International Journal of Epidemiology*, 35(4), 888–901.

Parents Involved in Community Schools v. Seattle School District, 551 U.S. 701 (2007).

Peters, S. J., Gentry, M., Whiting, G. W., & McBee, M. T. (2019). Who gets served in gifted education? Demographic representation and a call for action. *Gifted Child Quarterly*, 63(4), 273–287.

Petras, H., Masyn, K. E., Buckley, J. A., Ialongo, N. S., & Kellam, S. (2011). Who is most at risk for school removal? A multilevel discrete-time survival analysis of individual- and context-level influences.

Journal of Educational Psychology, 103(1), 223.

Reardon, S. F. (2016). School segregation and racial academic achievement gaps. *RSF: The Russell Sage Foundation Journal of the Social Sciences*, 2(5), 34–57.

Reed, D. S. (2014). *Building the federal schoolhouse: Localism and the American education state*. Oxford University Press.

Rosenbaum, J. (2020). Educational and criminal justice outcomes 12 years after school suspension. *Youth & Society*, 52(4), 515–547.

Ruell, P. (2016). For life expectancy, money matters. https://news.harvard.edu/gazette/story/2016/04/for-life-expectancy-money-matters/

Shollenberger, T. L. (2015). Racial disparities in school suspensions and subsequent outcomes. In D. J. Losen (Ed.), *Closing the school discipline gap: Equitable remedies for excessive exclusion* (pp. 31–43). Teachers College Press.

School Diversity Advisory Group. (2019). *Making the Grade II: New programs for better schools*. https://docs.wixstatic.com/ugd/1c478c_1d5659bd05494f6d-8cb2bbf03fcc95dd.pdf

Skiba, R. J. (2014). The failure of zero tolerance. *Reclaiming Children and Youth*, 22(4), 27.

Skiba, R. J. (2015). Interventions to address racial/ethnic disparities in school discipline: Can systems reform be race-neutral? In *Race and social problems* (pp. 107–124). Springer.

Skiba, R. J., & Knesting, K. (2002). Zero tolerance, zero evidence: An analysis of school disciplinary practice. In *Zero tolerance: Can suspension and expulsion keep school safe?* (pp. 17–43). Jossey-Bass/Wiley.

Skiba, R., & Peterson, R. (1999). The dark side of zero tolerance: Can punishment lead to safe schools? *The Phi Delta Kappan*, 80(5), 372–382.

St. George, D. (2011). *Suicide turns attention to Fairfax discipline procedures*. https://www.washingtonpost.com/wp-dyn/content/article/2011/02/19/AR2011021904141.html

Steele, C. (2010). *Whistling Vivaldi: And other clues to how stereotypes affect us* (1st ed.). W.W. Norton and Company.

Suh, S., Malchow, A., & Suh, J. (2014). Why did the Black-White dropout gap widen in the 2000s? *Educational Research Quarterly, 37*(4), 19–40.

Sumner, M. D., Silverman, C. J., & Frampton, M. L. (2010). *School-based restorative justice as an alternative to zero-tolerance policies: Lessons from West Oakland.* University of California, Berkeley, School of Law: Thelton E. Henderson Center for Social Justice. Retrieved from https://www.law.berkeley.edu/files/thcsj/10-2010_School-based_Restorative_Justice_As_an_Alternative_to_Zero-Tolerance_Policies.pdf

Theokas, C., & Saaris, R. (2013). *Finding America's missing AP and IB students.* Shattering expectations series. Education Trust.

Thomas, D., & Fry, R. (2020, November 30). *Prior to COVID-19, child poverty rates had reached record lows in U.S.* https://www.pewresearch.org/fact-tank/2020/11/30/prior-to-covid-19-child-poverty-rates-had-reached-record-lows-in-u-s/

Trump delivers remarks from the National Archives Museum in Washington. (2020). Youtube. https://youtu.be/zMQdHCCsrYE

Ture, K., Carmichael, S., & Hamilton, C. V. (1967). *Black power: The politics of liberation in America* (Vol. 33). Vintage.

Tyson, K. (2011). *Integration interrupted: Tracking, Black students, and acting White after Brown.* Oxford University Press.

Tyson, K. (2013). Tracking segregation, and the opportunity gap. *Closing the opportunity gap: What America must do to give every child an even chance,* 169–180.

U.S. Department of Education. (2021). *Condition of Education.* Racial/Ethnic enrollment in public schools.

Vavrus, F., & Cole, K. (2002). "I didn't do nothin'": The discursive construction of school suspension. *The Urban Review, 34*(2), 87–111.

Vogl, K., & Preckel, F. (2014). Full-time ability grouping of gifted students: Impacts on social self-concept and school-related attitudes. *Gifted Child Quarterly, 58*(1), 51–68.

Wallace, J. M., Goodkind, S., Wallace, C. M., & Bachman, J. G. (2008). Racial, ethnic, and gender differences in school discipline among U.S. high school students: 1991–2005. *The Negro Educational Review, 59*(1–2), 47–62.

Welsh, R. O., & Little, S. (2018). The school discipline dilemma: A comprehensive review of disparities and alternative approaches. *Review of Educational Research, 88*(5), 752–794.

Werblow, J., Urick, A., & Duesbery, L. (2013). On the wrong track: How tracking is associated with dropping out of high school. *Equity & Excellence in Education, 46*(2), 270–284. https://doi.org/10.1080/10665684.2013.779168

Wilson, J. L., Slate, J. R., Moore, G. W., & Barnes, W. (2014). *Advanced placement scores for Black male students from Connecticut, Florida, Maryland, Massachetts, and Texas.* Education Research International.

Index

Keep learning...

Gregory C. Hutchings, Jr.

Revolutionary Ed, LLC

Founded by Dr. Gregory C. Hutchings, Jr., Revolutionary Ed, LLC is an educational consulting firm with a mission to support and empower school systems, higher education institutions, and organizations to achieve true systemic transformational change that has a positive and sustainable impact on the social, emotional, and academic learning of every learner as well as dismantling systemic racism through unapologetic implementation of antiracist practices.

www.revolutionary-ed.com

Douglas S. Reed

Rose Hill Education Associates

Headed by Dr. Douglas S. Reed, Rose Hill Education Associates offers analysis and consulting in both preK–12 and higher education environments, with strengths in school finance, equity analysis, organizational change, and strategic analysis of equity goals, objectives, and obstacles.

Click on the Rose Hill tab at **douglas-reed.com** for more information.

A SAGE Publishing Company

Helping educators make the greatest impact

CORWIN HAS ONE MISSION: to enhance education through intentional professional learning.

We build long-term relationships with our authors, educators, clients, and associations who partner with us to develop and continuously improve the best evidence-based practices that establish and support lifelong learning.